# The Lastest

# Air Fryer

# Cookbook

# UK

600 Days Easy and Flavorful Air Fryer Recipes for the Whole Family From Beginners to Advanced Users 2023 Edition

**Ladarius Rolfson**

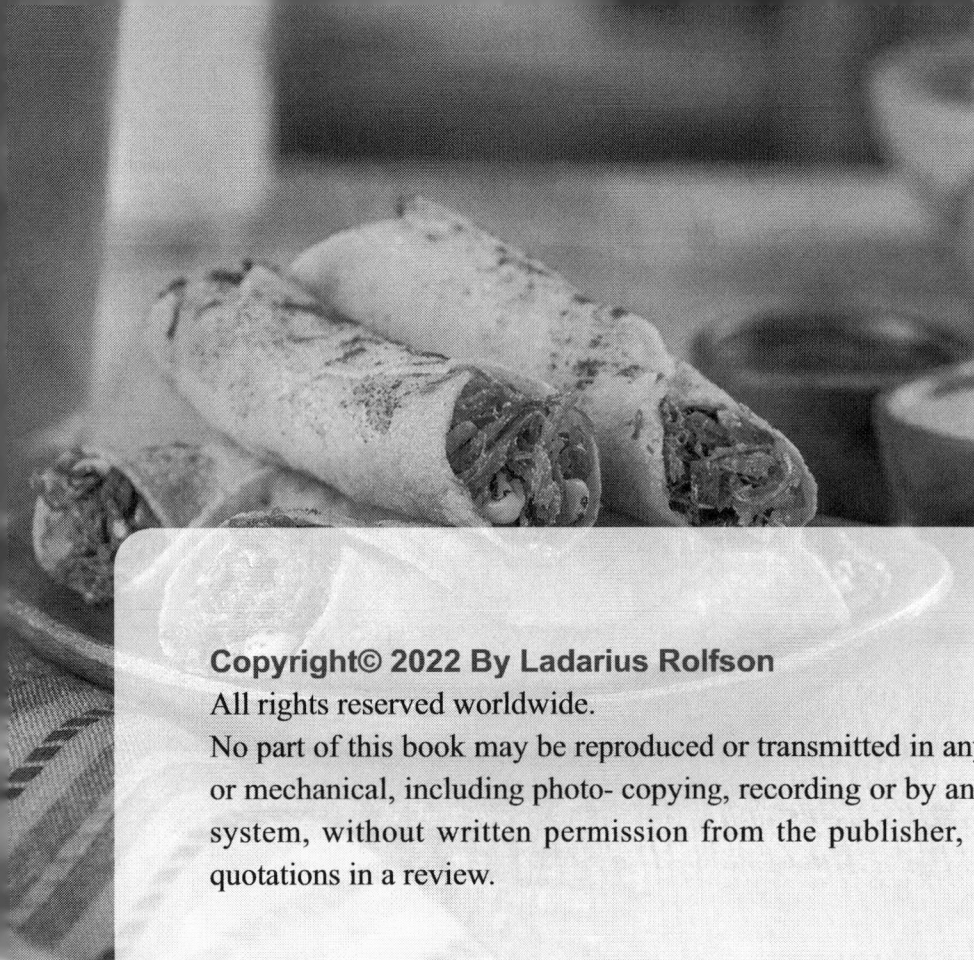

**Warning-Disclaimer**

The purpose of this book is to educate and entertain. The author or publisher does not guarantee that anyone following the techniques, suggestions, tips, ideas, or strategies will become successful. The author and publisher shall have neither liability or responsibility to anyone with respect to any loss or damage caused, or alleged to be caused, directly or indirectly by the information contained in this book.

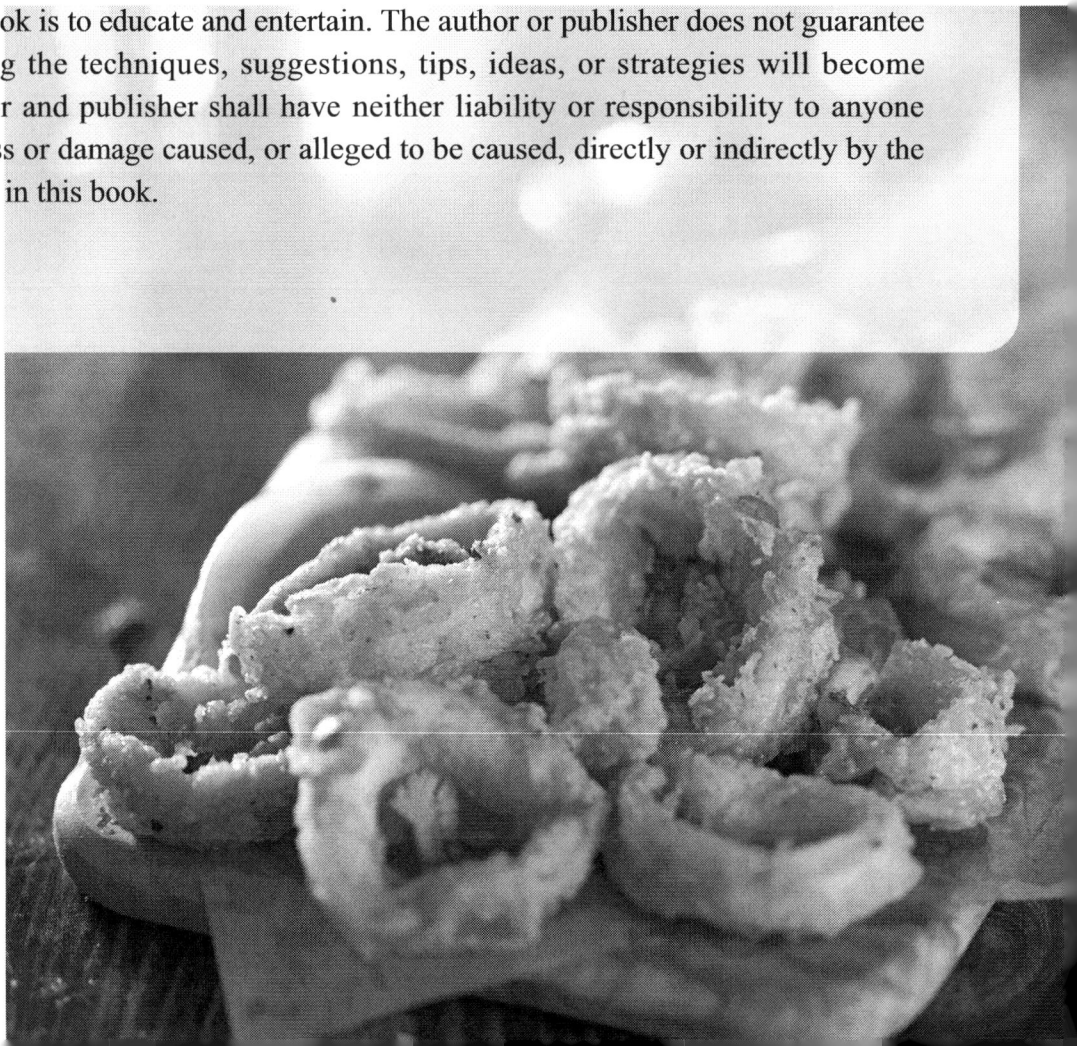

# Table of Contents

Table of Contents

## Chapter 5 Fish and Seafood                                                  33

## Chapter 6 Fast and Easy Everyday Favourites                                41

# INTRODUCTION

It's easy to fall in love with cooking using the right tools and ingredients. An air fryer helps reduce the fat and calories found in fried food while maintaining that crisp, crunchy texture we all know and love.

Being someone passionate about cooking myself, I have used an Air Fryer for just about a year. I have found it to be an excellent kitchen appliance that substantially reduces cooking time and, more importantly, allows me to cook the most delicious meals that always manage to please those served!

With its exceptional qualities, it's no wonder this appliance has been swiftly taking over kitchens worldwide! The combination of great results with ease of cooking – something that I have personally experienced in the time I have used it – makes air fryers a favourite among consumers—which is the primary reason for their global popularity.

Honestly, they're exactly what they are described as! Deep-fried food doesn't only come with frying oil, but you also have plenty of dishes to clean up after cooking. Plus, preventing yourself from the risk of getting burned is a whole different story with conventional deep-fried cooking!

And that's where these magical appliances come in; they let you cook traditionally deep-fried food, like chicken wings and french fries, with no additional ingredients (such as oil). It might sound too good to be true, but trust me, it isn't; I have first-hand experience with it myself!

Air frying works wonders for intricate dishes, especially those that typically take ages to make. You're probably wondering what kind of delicious dishes you can make with an air fryer. I'm going to show you how to maximise your air fryers' potential, so stick around!

The cookbook we have designed has all the magic a cook would want! From easy recipes that can be implemented by novice cooks (who have just started their cooking journey) to more advanced ones that require a little more experience, you can rest assured that our cookbook will have something for you!

The cookbook that comes with an Air fryer is designed to give you all the information you need to use it correctly. Plus, it has a lot of recipes and tips on cooking everything from cheesecake to steak in your air fryer.

No matter how experienced or inexperienced an air fryer cook you are (or think you are), this book is bound to have something for everyone! So kick back, grab a favourite recipe, and start cooking some excellent food today!

# Chapter 1 The Ultimate Guide to the Perfect Air Fryer

An air fryer is similar to an oven because it bakes and roasts, but what sets it apart is its heating elements which are only at the top rather than being placed all around.

Combined with a powerful fan, this results in food that stays crispier without too much oil, perfect for those who want to stay healthy while still indulging in some fast bites!

If you love deep-fried food but hate the excess fat, then an air fryer may be the kitchen gadget your life requires! Air fryers use 75% less oil than conventional cooking methods and make your favourite meals crispy and crunchy without making them soggy or greasy.

Plus, unlike other cooking methods, air fryers can actually cook frozen food in record time! Read on to learn about these five surprising benefits of using an air fryer!

# Surprising Benefits of Using an Air Fryer

### Less Fat

The most critical factor for most people buying an air fryer is the potential for healthier cooking. With very little oil used in the cooking process, this is a perfect way to replace deeply fried food that is not healthy with a healthier alternative.

You still need to coat fried food (like breaded chicken tenders and deep-fried fish) with a bit of oil for the breading to get evenly crispy as it cooks. Since there's no hot bubbling pot of oil over high heat frying them, french fries and tater tots will also get an excellent crisp result without much deep-frying.

### Faster Meals

Another major perk of an air fryer is that it heats up in seconds, and the circulation of heated air ensures even cooking - without much involvement from your end. This allows users to prepare food much quicker than the prep time taken in ovens, which requires much extra time, especially since preheating is necessary.

Since an average-sized kitchen has enough room for a stovetop but rarely has space for two appliances, this wayward appliance is a great boon for those with limited space on their countertops or pantry shelves.

### More Meal Choices

The air fryer is more than a healthier option for deep frying. You can cook literally anything in this appliance—from fried chicken and whole spaghetti squash to curries, desserts and everything in between. It's also perfect for baking frozen store-bought food like french fries, tater tots, and pizzas! This allows kids to prepare their food for themselves, too, as long as they are careful!

### Less Energy

There are many good reasons to love an air fryer, but one reason, in particular, makes it worth every penny and second. Your energy bills will be significantly lower because air frying machines use less energy than large ovens; they also cook food quicker, so your time spent cooking will also go down drastically! All this equals a lower monthly utility bill if you switch to an air fryer instead of regularly opting for larger ovens.

### Easy To Clean

Cleaning up after cooking is no one's favourite thing, but it does bring with it some sense of satisfaction.

This also applies to air fryers; if you are diligent about keeping them clean, they're straightforward to take care of!

You can keep them tidy by adding soapy water to the basket and using a non-scratch sponge to clean the interior and exterior. Some baskets can even go in the dishwasher; follow the instructions on your model carefully!

You must deep-clean these units periodically (depending on the frequency of usage) by giving both the cooking coil and body a thorough clean——about once or twice per month should suffice!

# Different Types of Air Fryers

There are different types of air fryers in the market today, and choosing the best one can be tricky. To help, we've put together this list of five different kinds of air fryers that should give you some options to consider if you're in the market for one soon. Whether you want to buy online or in-store, these air fryers are sure to please.

### Basket Air Fryers

The most popular type of air fryer is the basket variety. For convenience, air fryers with a basket are easy to fill, insert, and remove. However, these appliances require you to shake or stir the ingredients halfway through the cooking process so that they cook evenly - this can be inconvenient if you don't have time. Before buying a basket air fryer, make sure it has a large enough capacity for what you're planning to use it for!

### Paddle Air Fryers

Paddle Air fryers come fitted with paddles, which can mix up the contents in the cooking trays or baskets. This reduces the need for shaking or stirring food while they cook and offer a more comfortable way of cooking than traditional methods.

### Air Fryer Toaster Ovens

Although all air fryers are based on conventional ovens, some have evolved into something between them. Manufacturers created electric ovens with more power and fans to offer a similar function to air frying.

Some newer models can air fry food while holding traditional functions like baking, broiling and toasting. You can grill items without a grill with an air fryer toaster oven, which is perfect for condominium living. Air fryer toaster ovens typically go up to 450-500 degrees Fahrenheit and will give your food the nice charr or even grill marks when cooking - just like the Air Fryer BBQ Pork Tenderloin.

### Multi-purpose Air Fryers

Multi-purpose air fryers offer convenience because they can replace multiple items in the kitchen. Not only that but some of these products are also slow cookers and pressure cookers—all in one!

The air fryer part is located in the lid, with the rest being a traditional slow cooker. Now there are even multi-purpose air fryers that act as microwaves and steamers too! While this may sound great, remember that only some features will work.

### Specialty Air Fryers

Speciality fryers are designed for cooking specific food that can't be cooked in regular ovens or microwaves. Most common examples include turkey fryers which are made for roasting whole turkeys. However, these appliances will collect dust on your countertop unless you often roast turkeys or chickens.

## Air Fryer Cooking Tips

Always keep the grate in the basket.

This way, heat circulates and cooks food evenly without getting drenched with grease or sitting for too long.

It's hands-on.

You must take the basket out and shuffle the food around every few minutes for browning purposes.

Food cooks quickly - far quicker than you are used to!

And this is one of the best features of the air fryer. Your air fryer's instruction manual likely has a convenient table listing cooking times and temperatures for familiar food. When there is less food inside, the cooking time will be shorter; when more items are in your basket, this process will take longer.

It's permissible to take a peak at the cooking process anytime during cooking.

There is no need to turn off the machine or remove the basket - it will switch off automatically once it senses that there isn't anything in there anymore.

## FAQs

What Air Fryer Should I Buy?

Air fryers come in all sizes, so it depends on your needs and the needs of the people you cook for. For example, I recommend 5.8qt for smaller families or college students, but if you are cooking for a big group, try out Tower T10721 Air Fryer, which can cook up to 10 pounds at once!

Can I Use Oil in an Air Fryer?

Yes, it's possible to use oil in an Air Fryer. Though many people think that cooking requires little to no oil when using an Air Fryer, this is true for some recipes. Some recipes - like those with breaded goods such as french fries made from scratch - will require some olive or vegetable oil for crispy edges, just like deep-fried goods.

Why Does My Air Fryer Smell Like Plastic?

This happens because of the plastics used in the design of the air fryer baskets. The heat releases the new-air-fryer odour; most of the time, just washing it with soap and water before first use will take care of this.

Do Air Fryers Take a Lot of Electricity?

Air fryers use less energy than common appliances such as ovens or microwaves.

# Chapter 2 Breakfasts

## Bacon Cheese Egg with Avocado

**Prep time: 15 minutes | Cook time: 20 minutes | Serves 4**

6 large eggs
60 ml double cream
350 ml chopped cauliflower
235 ml shredded medium
Cheddar cheese
1 medium avocado, peeled and
pitted

8 tablespoons full-fat sour
cream
2 spring onions, sliced on the
bias
12 slices bacon, cooked and
crumbled

In a medium bowl, whisk eggs and cream together. Pour into a round baking dish. Add cauliflower and mix, then top with Cheddar. Place dish into the air fryer basket. Adjust the temperature to 160ºC and set the timer for 20 minutes. When completely cooked, eggs will be firm and cheese will be browned. Slice into four pieces. Slice avocado and divide evenly among pieces. Top each piece with 2 tablespoons sour cream, sliced spring onions, and crumbled bacon.

## Breakfast Meatballs

**Prep time: 10 minutes | Cook time: 15 minutes |**
**Makes 18 meatballs**

450 g pork sausage meat,
removed from casings
½ teaspoon salt
¼ teaspoon ground black
pepper

120 ml shredded sharp Cheddar
cheese
30 g cream cheese, softened
1 large egg, whisked

Combine all ingredients in a large bowl. Form mixture into eighteen 1-inch meatballs. Place meatballs into ungreased air fryer basket. Adjust the temperature to 200ºC and air fry for 15 minutes, shaking basket three times during cooking. Meatballs will be browned on the outside and have an internal temperature of at least 65ºC when completely cooked. Serve warm.

## Sausage and Egg Breakfast Burrito

**Prep time: 5 minutes | Cook time: 30 minutes | Serves 6**

6 eggs
Salt and pepper, to taste
Cooking oil
120 ml chopped red pepper
120 ml chopped green pepper
230 g chicken sausage meat

(removed from casings)
120 ml salsa
6 medium (8-inch) flour tortillas
120 ml shredded Cheddar
cheese

In a medium bowl, whisk the eggs. Add salt and pepper to taste. Place a skillet on medium-high heat. Spray with cooking oil. Add the eggs. Scramble for 2 to 3 minutes, until the eggs are fluffy. Remove the eggs from the skillet and set aside. If needed, spray the skillet with more oil. Add the chopped red and green bell peppers. Cook for 2 to 3 minutes, until the peppers are soft. Add the sausage meat to the skillet. Break the sausage into smaller pieces using a spatula or spoon. Cook for 3 to 4 minutes, until the sausage is brown. Add the salsa and scrambled eggs. Stir to combine. Remove the skillet from heat. Spoon the mixture evenly onto the tortillas. To form the burritos, fold the sides of each tortilla in toward the middle and then roll up from the bottom. You can secure each burrito with a toothpick. Or you can moisten the outside edge of the tortilla with a small amount of water. I prefer to use a cooking brush, but you can also dab with your fingers. Spray the burritos with cooking oil and place them in the air fryer. Do not stack. Cook the burritos in batches if they do not all fit in the basket. Air fry at 200ºC for 8 minutes. Open the air fryer and flip the burritos. Cook for an additional 2 minutes or until crisp. 1If necessary, repeat steps 8 and 9 for the remaining burritos. 1Sprinkle the Cheddar cheese over the burritos. Cool before serving.

## Sausage and Cheese Balls

**Prep time: 10 minutes | Cook time: 12 minutes |**
**Makes 16 balls**

450 g pork sausage meat,
removed from casings
120 ml shredded Cheddar
cheese

30 g full-fat cream cheese,
softened
1 large egg

Mix all ingredients in a large bowl. Form into sixteen (1-inch) balls. Place the balls into the air fryer basket. Adjust the temperature to 200ºC and air fry for 12 minutes. Shake the basket two or three times during cooking. Sausage balls will be browned on the outside and have an internal temperature of at least 65ºC when completely cooked. Serve warm.

## Jalapeño Popper Egg Cups

**Prep time: 10 minutes | Cook time: 10 minutes | Serves 2**

4 large eggs
60 ml chopped pickled
jalapeños

60 g full-fat cream cheese
120 ml shredded sharp Cheddar
cheese

In a medium bowl, beat the eggs, then pour into four silicone muffin cups. In a large microwave-safe bowl, place jalapeños, cream cheese, and Cheddar. Microwave for 30 seconds and stir. Take a spoonful, approximately ¼ of the mixture, and place it in the center of one of the egg cups. Repeat with remaining mixture. Place egg cups into the air fryer basket. Adjust the temperature to 160ºC and bake for 10 minutes. Serve warm.

## Kale and Potato Nuggets

**Prep time: 10 minutes | Cook time: 18 minutes | Serves 4**

| | |
|---|---|
| 1 teaspoon extra virgin olive oil | 30 ml milk |
| 1 clove garlic, minced | Salt and ground black pepper, |
| 1 L kale, rinsed and chopped | to taste |
| 475 ml potatoes, boiled and mashed | Cooking spray |

Preheat the air fryer to 200°C. In a skillet over medium heat, sauté the garlic in the olive oil, until it turns golden brown. Sauté with the kale for an additional 3 minutes and remove from the heat. Mix the mashed potatoes, kale and garlic in a bowl. Pour in the milk and sprinkle with salt and pepper. Shape the mixture into nuggets and spritz with cooking spray. Put in the air fryer basket and air fry for 15 minutes, flip the nuggets halfway through cooking to make sure the nuggets fry evenly. Serve immediately.

## Asparagus and Bell Pepper Strata

**Prep time: 10 minutes | Cook time: 14 to 20 minutes**

**| Serves 4**

| | |
|---|---|
| 8 large asparagus spears, trimmed and cut into 2-inch pieces | into ½-inch cubes |
| | 3 egg whites |
| 80 ml shredded carrot | 1 egg |
| 120 ml chopped red pepper | 3 tablespoons 1% milk |
| 2 slices wholemeal bread, cut | ½ teaspoon dried thyme |

In a baking pan, combine the asparagus, carrot, red bell pepper, and 1 tablespoon of water. Bake in the air fryer at 165°C for 3 to 5 minutes, or until crisp-tender. Drain well. Add the bread cubes to the vegetables and gently toss. In a medium bowl, whisk the egg whites, egg, milk, and thyme until frothy. Pour the egg mixture into the pan. Bake for 11 to 15 minutes, or until the strata is slightly puffy and set and the top starts to brown. Serve.

## Greek Bagels

**Prep time: 10 minutes | Cook time: 10 minutes | Makes 2**

**bagels**

| | |
|---|---|
| 120 ml self-raising flour, plus more for dusting | 4 teaspoons sesame seeds or za'atar |
| 120 ml plain Greek yoghurt | Cooking oil spray |
| 1 egg | 1 tablespoon butter, melted |
| 1 tablespoon water | |

In a large bowl, using a wooden spoon, stir together the flour and yoghurt until a tacky dough forms. Transfer the dough to a lightly floured work surface and roll the dough into a ball. Cut the dough into 2 pieces and roll each piece into a log. Form each log into a bagel shape, pinching the ends together. In a small bowl, whisk the egg and water. Brush the egg wash on the bagels. Sprinkle 2 teaspoons of the toppings on each bagel and gently press it into the dough. Insert the crisper plate into the basket and the basket into the unit. Preheat the unit by selecting BAKE, setting the temperature

to 165°C, and setting the time to 3 minutes. Select START/STOP to begin. Once the unit is preheated, spray the crisper plate with cooking spray. Drizzle the bagels with the butter and place them into the basket. Select BAKE, set the temperature to 165°C, and set the time to 10 minutes. Select START/STOP to begin. When the cooking is complete, the bagels should be lightly golden on the outside. Serve warm.

## Potatoes Lyonnaise

**Prep time: 10 minutes | Cook time: 31 minutes | Serves 4**

| | |
|---|---|
| 1 sweet/mild onion, sliced | thick |
| 1 teaspoon butter, melted | 1 tablespoon vegetable oil |
| 1 teaspoon brown sugar | Salt and freshly ground black |
| 2 large white potatoes (about 450 g in total), sliced ½-inch | pepper, to taste |

Preheat the air fryer to 190°C. Toss the sliced onions, melted butter and brown sugar together in the air fryer basket. Air fry for 8 minutes, shaking the basket occasionally to help the onions cook evenly. While the onions are cooking, bring a saucepan of salted water to a boil on the stovetop. Par-cook the potatoes in boiling water for 3 minutes. Drain the potatoes and pat them dry with a clean kitchen towel. Add the potatoes to the onions in the air fryer basket and drizzle with vegetable oil. Toss to coat the potatoes with the oil and season with salt and freshly ground black pepper. Increase the air fryer temperature to 200°C and air fry for 20 minutes, tossing the vegetables a few times during the cooking time to help the potatoes brown evenly. Season with salt and freshly ground black pepper and serve warm.

## Lemon-Blueberry Muffins

**Prep time: 5 minutes | Cook time: 20 to 25 minutes |**

**Makes 6**

| muffins | |
|---|---|
| 300 ml almond flour | 2 large eggs |
| 3 tablespoons granulated sweetener | 3 tablespoons melted butter |
| | 1 tablespoon almond milk |
| 1 teaspoon baking powder | 1 tablespoon fresh lemon juice |
| | 120 ml fresh blueberries |

Preheat the air fryer to 175°C. Lightly coat 6 silicone muffin cups with vegetable oil. Set aside. In a large mixing bowl, combine the almond flour, sweetener, and baking soda. Set aside. In a separate small bowl, whisk together the eggs, butter, milk, and lemon juice. Add the egg mixture to the flour mixture and stir until just combined. Fold in the blueberries and let the batter sit for 5 minutes. Spoon the muffin batter into the muffin cups, about two-thirds full. Air fry for 20 to 25 minutes, or until a toothpick inserted into the center of a muffin comes out clean. Remove the basket from the air fryer and let the muffins cool for about 5 minutes before transferring them to a wire rack to cool completely.

## Spinach and Swiss Frittata with Mushrooms

**Prep time: 10 minutes | Cook time: 20 minutes | Serves 4**

Olive oil cooking spray
8 large eggs
½ teaspoon salt
½ teaspoon black pepper
1 garlic clove, minced
475 ml fresh baby spinach

110 g baby mushrooms, sliced
1 shallot, diced
120 ml shredded Swiss cheese, divided
Hot sauce, for serving (optional)

Preheat the air fryer to 180ºC. Lightly coat the inside of a 6-inch round cake pan with olive oil cooking spray. In a large bowl, beat the eggs, salt, pepper, and garlic for 1 to 2 minutes, or until well combined. Fold in the spinach, mushrooms, shallot, and 60 ml the Swiss cheese. Pour the egg mixture into the prepared cake pan, and sprinkle the remaining 60 ml Swiss over the top. Place into the air fryer and bake for 18 to 20 minutes, or until the eggs are set in the center. Remove from the air fryer and allow to cool for 5 minutes. Drizzle with hot sauce (if using) before serving.

## Cheddar Soufflés

**Prep time: 15 minutes | Cook time: 12 minutes | Serves 4**

3 large eggs, whites and yolks separated
¼ teaspoon cream of tartar

120 ml shredded sharp Cheddar cheese
85 g cream cheese, softened

In a large bowl, beat egg whites together with cream of tartar until soft peaks form, about 2 minutes. In a separate medium bowl, beat egg yolks, Cheddar, and cream cheese together until frothy, about 1 minute. Add egg yolk mixture to whites, gently folding until combined. Pour mixture evenly into four ramekins greased with cooking spray. Place ramekins into air fryer basket. Adjust the temperature to 175ºC and bake for 12 minutes. Eggs will be browned on the top and firm in the center when done. Serve warm.

## Keto Quiche

**Prep time: 10 minutes | Cook time: 1 hour | Makes 1 (6-inch) quiche**

Crust:
300 ml blanched almond flour
300 ml grated Parmesan or Gouda cheese
¼ teaspoon fine sea salt
1 large egg, beaten
Filling:
120 ml chicken or beef stock (or vegetable stock for vegetarian)
235 ml shredded Swiss cheese (about 110 g)

110 g cream cheese (120 ml)
1 tablespoon unsalted butter, melted
4 large eggs, beaten
80 ml minced leeks or sliced spring onions
¾ teaspoon fine sea salt
⅛ teaspoon cayenne pepper
Chopped spring onions, for garnish

Preheat the air fryer to 165ºC. Grease a pie pan. Spray two large pieces of parchment paper with avocado oil and set them on the countertop. Make the crust: In a medium-sized bowl, combine the flour, cheese, and salt and mix well. Add the egg and mix until the dough is well combined and stiff. Place the dough in the center of one of the greased pieces of parchment. Top with the other piece of parchment. Using a rolling pin, roll out the dough into a circle about 1/16 inch thick. Press the pie crust into the prepared pie pan. Place it in the air fryer and bake for 12 minutes, or until it starts to lightly brown. While the crust bakes, make the filling: In a large bowl, combine the stock, Swiss cheese, cream cheese, and butter. Stir in the eggs, leeks, salt, and cayenne pepper. When the crust is ready, pour the mixture into the crust. Place the quiche in the air fryer and bake for 15 minutes. Turn the heat down to 150ºC and bake for an additional 30 minutes, or until a knife inserted 1 inch from the edge comes out clean. You may have to cover the edges of the crust with foil to prevent burning. Allow the quiche to cool for 10 minutes before garnishing it with chopped spring onions and cutting it into wedges. Store leftovers in an airtight container in the refrigerator for up to 4 days or in the freezer for up to a month. Reheat in a preheated 175ºC air fryer for a few minutes, until warmed through.

## Three-Berry Dutch Pancake

**Prep time: 10 minutes | Cook time: 12 to 16 minutes | Serves 4**

2 egg whites
1 egg
120 ml wholemeal plain flour plus 1 tablespoon cornflour
120 ml semi-skimmed milk
1 teaspoon pure vanilla extract

1 tablespoon unsalted butter, melted
235 ml sliced fresh strawberries
120 ml fresh blueberries
120 ml fresh raspberries

In a medium bowl, use an eggbeater or hand mixer to quickly mix the egg whites, egg, flour, milk, and vanilla until well combined. Use a pastry brush to grease the bottom of a baking pan with the melted butter. Immediately pour in the batter and put the basket back in the fryer. Bake at 165ºC for 12 to 16 minutes, or until the pancake is puffed and golden brown. Remove the pan from the air fryer; the pancake will fall. Top with the strawberries, blueberries, and raspberries. Serve immediately.

## Onion Omelette

**Prep time: 10 minutes | Cook time: 12 minutes | Serves 2**

3 eggs
Salt and ground black pepper, to taste
½ teaspoons soy sauce

1 large onion, chopped
2 tablespoons grated Cheddar cheese
Cooking spray

Preheat the air fryer to 180ºC. In a bowl, whisk together the eggs, salt, pepper, and soy sauce. Spritz a small pan with cooking spray. Spread the chopped onion across the bottom of the pan, then transfer the pan to the air fryer. Bake in the preheated air fryer for 6 minutes or until the onion is translucent. Add the egg mixture on top of the onions to coat well. Add the cheese on top, then continue baking for another 6 minutes. Allow to cool before serving.

## Poached Eggs on Whole Grain Avocado Toast

**Prep time: 5 minutes | Cook time: 7 minutes | Serves 4**

| | |
|---|---|
| Olive oil cooking spray | 4 pieces wholegrain bread |
| 4 large eggs | 1 avocado |
| Salt | Red pepper flakes (optional) |
| Black pepper | |

Preheat the air fryer to 160ºC. Lightly coat the inside of four small oven-safe ramekins with olive oil cooking spray. Crack one egg into each ramekin, and season with salt and black pepper. Place the ramekins into the air fryer basket. Close and set the timer to 7 minutes. While the eggs are cooking, toast the bread in a toaster. Slice the avocado in half lengthwise, remove the pit, and scoop the flesh into a small bowl. Season with salt, black pepper, and red pepper flakes, if desired. Using a fork, smash the avocado lightly. Spread a quarter of the smashed avocado evenly over each slice of toast. Remove the eggs from the air fryer, and gently spoon one onto each slice of avocado toast before serving.

## Butternut Squash and Ricotta Frittata

**Prep time: 10 minutes | Cook time: 33 minutes | Serves 2 to 3**

| | |
|---|---|
| 235 ml cubed (½-inch) butternut squash (160 g) | 4 fresh sage leaves, thinly sliced |
| 2 tablespoons olive oil | 6 large eggs, lightly beaten |
| Coarse or flaky salt and freshly ground black pepper, to taste | 120 ml ricotta cheese |
| | Cayenne pepper |

In a bowl, toss the squash with the olive oil and season with salt and black pepper until evenly coated. Sprinkle the sage on the bottom of a cake pan and place the squash on top. Place the pan in the air fryer and bake at 200ºC for 10 minutes. Stir to incorporate the sage, then cook until the squash is tender and lightly caramelized at the edges, about 3 minutes more. Pour the eggs over the squash, dollop the ricotta all over, and sprinkle with cayenne. Bake at 150ºC until the eggs are set and the frittata is golden brown on top, about 20 minutes. Remove the pan from the air fryer and cut the frittata into wedges to serve.

## Homemade Toaster Pastries

**Prep time: 10 minutes | Cook time: 11 minutes | Makes 6 pastries**

| | |
|---|---|
| Oil, for spraying | 475 ml icing sugar |
| 1 (425 g) package refrigerated piecrust | 3 tablespoons milk |
| 6 tablespoons jam or preserves of choice | 1 to 2 tablespoons sprinkles of choice |

Preheat the air fryer to 175ºC. Line the air fryer basket with parchment and spray lightly with oil. Cut the piecrust into 12 rectangles, about 3 by 4 inches each. You will need to reroll the dough scraps to get 12 rectangles. Spread 1 tablespoon of jam in the center of 6 rectangles, leaving ¼ inch around the edges. Pour some water into a small bowl. Use your finger to moisten the edge of each rectangle. Top each rectangle with another and use your fingers to press around the edges. Using the tines of a fork, seal the edges of the dough and poke a few holes in the top of each one. Place the pastries in the prepared basket. Air fry for 11 minutes. Let cool completely. In a medium bowl, whisk together the icing sugar and milk. Spread the icing over the tops of the pastries and add sprinkles. Serve immediately.

## Wholemeal Banana-Walnut Bread

**Prep time: 10 minutes | Cook time: 23 minutes | Serves 6**

| | |
|---|---|
| Olive oil cooking spray | 2 tablespoons honey |
| 2 ripe medium bananas | 235 ml wholemeal flour |
| 1 large egg | ¼ teaspoon salt |
| 60 ml non-fat plain Greek yoghurt | ¼ teaspoon baking soda |
| 60 ml olive oil | ½ teaspoon ground cinnamon |
| ½ teaspoon vanilla extract | 60 ml chopped walnuts |

Preheat the air fryer to 180ºC. Lightly coat the inside of a 8-by-4-inch loaf pan with olive oil cooking spray. (Or use two 5 ½-by-3-inch loaf pans.) In a large bowl, mash the bananas with a fork. Add the egg, yoghurt, olive oil, vanilla, and honey. Mix until well combined and mostly smooth. Sift the wholemeal flour, salt, baking soda, and cinnamon into the wet mixture, then stir until just combined. Do not overmix. Gently fold in the walnuts. Pour into the prepared loaf pan and spread to distribute evenly. Place the loaf pan in the air fryer basket and bake for 20 to 23 minutes, or until golden brown on top and a toothpick inserted into the center comes out clean. Allow to cool for 5 minutes before serving.

## Mozzarella Bacon Calzones

**Prep time: 15 minutes | Cook time: 12 minutes | Serves 4**

| | |
|---|---|
| 2 large eggs | 60 g cream cheese, softened and broken into small pieces |
| 235 ml blanched finely ground almond flour | 4 slices cooked bacon, crumbled |
| 475 ml shredded Mozzarella cheese | |

Beat eggs in a small bowl. Pour into a medium nonstick skillet over medium heat and scramble. Set aside. In a large microwave-safe bowl, mix flour and Mozzarella. Add cream cheese to the bowl. Place bowl in microwave and cook 45 seconds on high to melt cheese, then stir with a fork until a soft dough ball forms. Cut a piece of parchment to fit air fryer basket. Separate dough into two sections and press each out into an 8-inch round. On half of each dough round, place half of the scrambled eggs and crumbled bacon. Fold the other side of the dough over and press to seal the edges. Place calzones on ungreased parchment and into air fryer basket. Adjust the temperature to 175ºC and set the timer for 12 minutes, turning calzones halfway through cooking. Crust will be golden and firm when done. Let calzones cool on a cooking rack 5 minutes before serving.

## Buffalo Egg Cups

**Prep time: 10 minutes | Cook time: 15 minutes | Serves 2**

4 large eggs
60 g full-fat cream cheese
2 tablespoons buffalo sauce
120 ml shredded sharp Cheddar cheese

Crack eggs into two ramekins. In a small microwave-safe bowl, mix cream cheese, buffalo sauce, and Cheddar. Microwave for 20 seconds and then stir. Place a spoonful into each ramekin on top of the eggs. Place ramekins into the air fryer basket. Adjust the temperature to 160ºC and bake for 15 minutes. Serve warm.

## Bacon, Cheese, and Avocado Melt

**Prep time: 5 minutes | Cook time: 3 to 5 minutes | Serves 2**

1 avocado
4 slices cooked bacon, chopped
2 tablespoons salsa
1 tablespoon double cream
60 ml shredded Cheddar cheese

Preheat the air fryer to 200ºC. Slice the avocado in half lengthwise and remove the stone. To ensure the avocado halves do not roll in the basket, slice a thin piece of skin off the base. In a small bowl, combine the bacon, salsa, and cream. Divide the mixture between the avocado halves and top with the cheese. Place the avocado halves in the air fryer basket and air fry for 3 to 5 minutes until the cheese has melted and begins to brown. Serve warm.

## Gyro Breakfast Patties with Tzatziki

**Prep time: 10 minutes | Cook time: 20 minutes per batch | Makes 16**

patties
Patties:
900 g lamb or beef mince
120 ml diced red onions
60 ml sliced black olives
2 tablespoons tomato sauce
1 teaspoon dried oregano leaves
2 cloves garlic, minced
1 teaspoon fine sea salt
Tzatziki:
235 ml full-fat sour cream
1 small cucumber, chopped
½ teaspoon fine sea salt
½ teaspoon garlic powder, or 1 clove garlic, minced
¼ teaspoon dried dill, or 1 teaspoon finely chopped fresh dill
For Garnish/Serving:
120 ml crumbled feta cheese (about 60 g)
Diced red onions
Sliced black olives
Sliced cucumbers

Preheat the air fryer to 175ºC. Place the lamb, onions, olives, tomato sauce, oregano, garlic, and salt in a large bowl. Mix well to combine the ingredients. Using your hands, form the mixture into sixteen 3-inch patties. Place about 5 of the patties in the air fryer and air fry for 20 minutes, flipping halfway through. Remove the patties and place them on a serving platter. Repeat with the remaining patties. While the patties cook, make the tzatziki: Place all the ingredients in a small bowl and stir well. Cover and store in the fridge until ready to serve. Garnish with ground black pepper before serving. Serve the patties with a dollop of tzatziki, a sprinkle of crumbled feta cheese, diced red onions, sliced black olives, and sliced cucumbers. Store leftovers in an airtight container in the refrigerator for up to 5 days or in the freezer for up to a month. Reheat the patties in a preheated 200ºC air fryer for a few minutes, until warmed through.

## Berry Muffins

**Prep time: 15 minutes | Cook time: 12 to 17 minutes | Makes 8**

muffins
315 ml plus 1 tablespoon plain flour, divided
60 ml granulated sugar
2 tablespoons light brown sugar
2 teaspoons baking powder
2 eggs
160 ml whole milk
80 ml neutral oil
235 ml mixed fresh berries

In a medium bowl, stir together 315 ml of flour, the granulated sugar, brown sugar, and baking powder until mixed well. In a small bowl, whisk the eggs, milk, and oil until combined. Stir the egg mixture into the dry ingredients just until combined. In another small bowl, toss the mixed berries with the remaining 1 tablespoon of flour until coated. Gently stir the berries into the batter. Double up 16 foil muffin cups to make 8 cups. Insert the crisper plate into the basket and the basket into the unit. Preheat the unit by selecting BAKE, setting the temperature to 155ºC, and setting the time to 3 minutes. Select START/STOP to begin. Once the unit is preheated, place 1 L into the basket and fill each three-quarters full with the batter. Select BAKE, set the temperature to 155ºC, and set the time for 17 minutes. Select START/STOP to begin. After about 12 minutes, check the muffins. If they spring back when lightly touched with your finger, they are done. If not, resume cooking. When the cooking is done, transfer the muffins to a wire rack to cool. 1Repeat steps 6, 7, and 8 with the remaining muffin cups and batter. 1Let the muffins cool for 10 minutes before serving.

## Cheddar-Ham-Corn Muffins

**Prep time: 10 minutes | Cook time: 6 to 8 minutes per batch | Makes 8 muffins**

180 ml cornmeal/polenta
60 ml flour
1½ teaspoons baking powder
¼ teaspoon salt
1 egg, beaten
2 tablespoons rapeseed oil
120 ml milk
120 ml shredded sharp Cheddar cheese
120 ml diced ham
8 foil muffin cups, liners removed and sprayed with cooking spray

Preheat the air fryer to 200ºC. In a medium bowl, stir together the cornmeal, flour, baking powder, and salt. Add egg, oil, and milk to dry ingredients and mix well. Stir in shredded cheese and diced ham. Divide batter among the muffin cups. Place 4 filled muffin cups in air fryer basket and bake for 5 minutes. Reduce temperature to 165ºC and bake for 1 to 2 minutes or until toothpick inserted in center of muffin comes out clean. Repeat steps 6 and 7 to cook remaining muffins.

## Cheesy Scrambled Eggs

**Prep time: 2 minutes | Cook time: 9 minutes | Serves 2**

1 teaspoon unsalted butter
2 large eggs
2 tablespoons milk
2 tablespoons shredded Cheddar
cheese
Salt and freshly ground black
pepper, to taste

Preheat the air fryer to 150°C. Place the butter in a baking pan and cook for 1 to 2 minutes, until melted. In a small bowl, whisk together the eggs, milk, and cheese. Season with salt and black pepper. Transfer the mixture to the pan. Cook for 3 minutes. Stir the eggs and push them toward the center of the pan. Cook for another 2 minutes, then stir again. Cook for another 2 minutes, until the eggs are just cooked. Serve warm.

## Breakfast Calzone

**Prep time: 15 minutes | Cook time: 15 minutes | Serves 4**

350 ml shredded Mozzarella
cheese
120 ml blanched finely ground
almond flour
30 g full-fat cream cheese
1 large whole egg
4 large eggs, scrambled
230 g cooked sausage meat,
removed from casings and
crumbled
8 tablespoons shredded mild
Cheddar cheese

In a large microwave-safe bowl, add Mozzarella, almond flour, and cream cheese. Microwave for 1 minute. Stir until the mixture is smooth and forms a ball. Add the egg and stir until dough forms. Place dough between two sheets of parchment and roll out to ¼-inch thickness. Cut the dough into four rectangles. Mix scrambled eggs and cooked sausage together in a large bowl. Divide the mixture evenly among each piece of dough, placing it on the lower half of the rectangle. Sprinkle each with 2 tablespoons Cheddar. Fold over the rectangle to cover the egg and meat mixture. Pinch, roll, or use a wet fork to close the edges completely. Cut a piece of parchment to fit your air fryer basket and place the calzones onto the parchment. Place parchment into the air fryer basket. Adjust the temperature to 190°C and air fry for 15 minutes. Flip the calzones halfway through the cooking time. When done, calzones should be golden in color. Serve immediately.

## Western Frittata

**Prep time: 10 minutes | Cook time: 19 minutes | Serves 1 to 2**

½ red or green pepper, cut into
½-inch chunks
1 teaspoon olive oil
3 eggs, beaten
60 ml grated Cheddar cheese
60 ml diced cooked ham
Salt and freshly ground black
pepper, to taste
1 teaspoon butter
1 teaspoon chopped fresh
parsley

Preheat the air fryer to 200°C. Toss the peppers with the olive oil and air fry for 6 minutes, shaking the basket once or twice during the cooking process to redistribute the ingredients. While the vegetables are cooking, beat the eggs well in a bowl, stir in the Cheddar cheese and ham, and season with salt and freshly ground black pepper. Add the air-fried peppers to this bowl when they have finished cooking. Place a cake pan into the air fryer basket with the butter using an aluminum sling to lower the pan into the basket. Air fry for 1 minute at 190°C to melt the butter. Remove the cake pan and rotate the pan to distribute the butter and grease the pan. Pour the egg mixture into the cake pan and return the pan to the air fryer, using the aluminum sling. Air fry at 190°C for 12 minutes, or until the frittata has puffed up and is lightly browned. Let the frittata sit in the air fryer for 5 minutes to cool to an edible temperature and set up. Remove the cake pan from the air fryer, sprinkle with parsley and serve immediately.

## All-in-One Toast

**Prep time: 10 minutes | Cook time: 10 minutes | Serves 1**

1 strip bacon, diced
1 slice 1-inch thick bread
1 egg
Salt and freshly ground black
pepper, to taste
60 ml grated Monterey Jack or
Chedday cheese

Preheat the air fryer to 200°C. Air fry the bacon for 3 minutes, shaking the basket once or twice while it cooks. Remove the bacon to a paper towel lined plate and set aside. Use a sharp paring knife to score a large circle in the middle of the slice of bread, cutting halfway through, but not all the way through to the cutting board. Press down on the circle in the center of the bread slice to create an indentation. Transfer the slice of bread, hole side up, to the air fryer basket. Crack the egg into the center of the bread, and season with salt and pepper. Adjust the air fryer temperature to 190°C and air fry for 5 minutes. Sprinkle the grated cheese around the edges of the bread, leaving the center of the yolk uncovered, and top with the cooked bacon. Press the cheese and bacon into the bread lightly to help anchor it to the bread and prevent it from blowing around in the air fryer. Air fry for one or two more minutes, just to melt the cheese and finish cooking the egg. Serve immediately.

## Cajun Breakfast Sausage

**Prep time: 10 minutes | Cook time: 15 to 20 minutes | Serves 8**

680 g 85% lean turkey mince
3 cloves garlic, finely chopped
¼ onion, grated
1 teaspoon Tabasco sauce
1 teaspoon Cajun seasoning
1 teaspoon dried thyme
½ teaspoon paprika
½ teaspoon cayenne

Preheat the air fryer to 190°C. In a large bowl, combine the turkey, garlic, onion, Tabasco, Cajun seasoning, thyme, paprika, and cayenne. Mix with clean hands until thoroughly combined. Shape into 16 patties, about ½ inch thick. (Wet your hands slightly if you find the sausage too sticky to handle.) Working in batches if necessary, arrange the patties in a single layer in the air fryer basket. Pausing halfway through the cooking time to flip the patties, air fry for 15 to 20 minutes until a thermometer inserted into the thickest portion registers 75°C.

## Parmesan Sausage Egg Muffins

**Prep time: 5 minutes | Cook time: 20 minutes | Serves 4**

170 g Italian-seasoned sausage, sliced
6 eggs
30 ml double cream
Salt and ground black pepper, to taste
85 g Parmesan cheese, grated

Preheat the air fryer to 175ºC. Grease a muffin pan. Put the sliced sausage in the muffin pan. Beat the eggs with the cream in a bowl and season with salt and pepper. Pour half of the mixture over the sausages in the pan. Sprinkle with cheese and the remaining egg mixture. Bake in the preheated air fryer for 20 minutes or until set. Serve immediately.

## Breakfast Sausage and Cauliflower

**Prep time: 5 minutes | Cook time: 45 minutes | Serves 4**

450 g sausage meat, cooked and crumbled
475 ml double/whipping cream
1 head cauliflower, chopped
235 ml grated Cheddar cheese,
plus more for topping
8 eggs, beaten
Salt and ground black pepper, to taste

Preheat the air fryer to 175ºC. In a large bowl, mix the sausage, cream, chopped cauliflower, cheese and eggs. Sprinkle with salt and ground black pepper. Pour the mixture into a greased casserole dish. Bake in the preheated air fryer for 45 minutes or until firm. Top with more Cheddar cheese and serve.

## Wholemeal Blueberry Muffins

**Prep time: 10 minutes | Cook time: 15 minutes | Serves 6**

Olive oil cooking spray
120 ml unsweetened applesauce
60 ml honey
120 ml non-fat plain Greek yoghurt
1 teaspoon vanilla extract
1 large egg
350 ml plus 1 tablespoon wholemeal, divided
½ teaspoon baking soda
½ teaspoon baking powder
½ teaspoon salt
120 ml blueberries, fresh or frozen

Preheat the air fryer to 180ºC. Lightly coat the inside of six silicone muffin cups or a six-cup muffin tin with olive oil cooking spray. In a large bowl, combine the applesauce, honey, yoghurt, vanilla, and egg and mix until smooth. Sift in 350 ml of the flour, the baking soda, baking powder, and salt into the wet mixture, then stir until just combined. In a small bowl, toss the blueberries with the remaining 1 tablespoon flour, then fold the mixture into the muffin batter. Divide the mixture evenly among the prepared muffin cups and place into the basket of the air fryer. Bake for 12 to 15 minutes, or until golden brown on top and a toothpick inserted into the middle of one of the muffins comes out clean. Allow to cool for 5 minutes before serving.

## Cauliflower Avocado Toast

**Prep time: 15 minutes | Cook time: 8 minutes |**
**Serves 2**

1 (40 g) steamer bag cauliflower
1 large egg
120 ml shredded Mozzarella cheese
1 ripe medium avocado
½ teaspoon garlic powder
¼ teaspoon ground black pepper

Cook cauliflower according to package instructions. Remove from bag and place into cheesecloth or clean towel to remove excess moisture. Place cauliflower into a large bowl and mix in egg and Mozzarella. Cut a piece of parchment to fit your air fryer basket. Separate the cauliflower mixture into two, and place it on the parchment in two mounds. Press out the cauliflower mounds into a ¼-inch-thick rectangle. Place the parchment into the air fryer basket. Adjust the temperature to 200ºC and set the timer for 8 minutes. Flip the cauliflower halfway through the cooking time. When the timer beeps, remove the parchment and allow the cauliflower to cool 5 minutes. Cut open the avocado and remove the pit. Scoop out the inside, place it in a medium bowl, and mash it with garlic powder and pepper. Spread onto the cauliflower. Serve immediately.

## Sirloin Steaks with Eggs

**Prep time: 8 minutes | Cook time: 14 minutes per**
**batch | Serves 4**

Cooking oil spray
4 (110 g) sirloin steaks
1 teaspoon granulated garlic, divided
1 teaspoon salt, divided
1 teaspoon freshly ground black pepper, divided
4 eggs
½ teaspoon paprika

Insert the crisper plate into the basket and the basket into the unit. Preheat the unit by selecting AIR FRY, setting the temperature to 180ºC, and setting the time to 3 minutes. Select START/STOP to begin. Once the unit is preheated, spray the crisper plate with cooking oil. Place 2 steaks into the basket; do not oil or season them at this time. Select AIR FRY, set the temperature to 180ºC, and set the time to 9 minutes. Select START/STOP to begin. After 5 minutes, open the unit and flip the steaks. Sprinkle each with ¼ teaspoon of granulated garlic, ¼ teaspoon of salt, and ¼ teaspoon of pepper. Resume cooking until the steaks register at least 65ºC on a food thermometer. When the cooking is complete, transfer the steaks to a plate and tent with aluminum foil to keep warm. Repeat steps 2, 3, and 4 with the remaining steaks. Spray 4 ramekins with olive oil. Crack 1 egg into each ramekin. Sprinkle the eggs with the paprika and remaining ½ teaspoon each of salt and pepper. Working in batches, place 2 ramekins into the basket. Select BAKE, set the temperature to 165ºC, and set the time to 5 minutes. Select START/STOP to begin. When the cooking is complete and the eggs are cooked to 70ºC, remove the ramekins and repeat step 7 with the remaining 2 ramekins. Serve the eggs with the steaks.

## Cinnamon Rolls

### Prep time: 10 minutes | Cook time: 20 minutes | Makes 12 rolls

| | |
|---|---|
| 600 ml shredded Mozzarella cheese | ½ teaspoon vanilla extract |
| 60 g cream cheese, softened | 120 ml icing sugar-style sweetener |
| 235 ml blanched finely ground almond flour | 1 tablespoon ground cinnamon |

In a large microwave-safe bowl, combine Mozzarella cheese, cream cheese, and flour. Microwave the mixture on high 90 seconds until cheese is melted. Add vanilla extract and sweetener, and mix 2 minutes until a dough forms. Once the dough is cool enough to work with your hands, about 2 minutes, spread it out into a 12 × 4-inch rectangle on ungreased parchment paper. Evenly sprinkle dough with cinnamon. Starting at the long side of the dough, roll lengthwise to form a log. Slice the log into twelve even pieces. Divide rolls between two ungreased round nonstick baking dishes. Place one dish into air fryer basket. Adjust the temperature to 190ºC and bake for 10 minutes. Cinnamon rolls will be done when golden around the edges and mostly firm. Repeat with second dish. Allow rolls to cool in dishes 10 minutes before serving.

## Hearty Blueberry Oatmeal

### Prep time: 10 minutes | Cook time: 25 minutes | Serves 6

| | |
|---|---|
| 350 ml quick oats | 1 teaspoon vanilla extract |
| 1¼ teaspoons ground cinnamon, divided | 1 egg, beaten |
| ½ teaspoon baking powder | 475 ml blueberries |
| Pinch salt | Olive oil |
| 235 ml unsweetened vanilla almond milk | 1½ teaspoons sugar, divided |
| 60 ml honey | 6 tablespoons low-fat whipped topping (optional) |

In a large bowl, mix together the oats, 1 teaspoon of cinnamon, baking powder, and salt. In a medium bowl, whisk together the almond milk, honey, vanilla and egg. Pour the liquid ingredients into the oats mixture and stir to combine. Fold in the blueberries. Lightly spray a baking pan with oil. Add half the blueberry mixture to the pan. Sprinkle ⅛ teaspoon of cinnamon and ½ teaspoon sugar over the top. Cover the pan with aluminum foil and place gently in the air fryer basket. Air fry at 180ºC for 20 minutes. Remove the foil and air fry for an additional 5 minutes. Transfer the mixture to a shallow bowl. Repeat with the remaining blueberry mixture, ½ teaspoon of sugar, and ⅛ teaspoon of cinnamon. 1To serve, spoon into bowls and top with whipped topping.

## Mexican Breakfast Pepper Rings

### Prep time: 5 minutes | Cook time: 10 minutes | Serves 4

| | |
|---|---|
| Olive oil | 4 eggs |
| 1 large red, yellow, or orange pepper, cut into four ¾-inch rings | Salt and freshly ground black pepper, to taste |
| | 2 teaspoons salsa |

Preheat the air fryer to 175ºC. Lightly spray a baking pan with olive oil. Place 2 bell pepper rings on the pan. Crack one egg into each bell pepper ring. Season with salt and black pepper. Spoon ½ teaspoon of salsa on top of each egg. Place the pan in the air fryer basket. Air fry until the yolk is slightly runny, 5 to 6 minutes or until the yolk is fully cooked, 8 to 10 minutes. Repeat with the remaining 2 pepper rings. Serve hot.

## Bacon and Spinach Egg Muffins

### Prep time: 7 minutes | Cook time: 12 to 14 minutes | Serves 6

| | |
|---|---|
| 6 large eggs | (optional) |
| 60 ml double (whipping) cream | 180 ml frozen chopped spinach, thawed and drained |
| ½ teaspoon sea salt | |
| ¼ teaspoon freshly ground black pepper | 4 strips cooked bacon, crumbled |
| ¼ teaspoon cayenne pepper | 60 g shredded Cheddar cheese |

In a large bowl (with a spout if you have one), whisk together the eggs, double cream, salt, black pepper, and cayenne pepper (if using). Divide the spinach and bacon among 6 silicone muffin cups. Place the muffin cups in your air fryer basket. Divide the egg mixture among the muffin cups. Top with the cheese. Set the air fryer to 150ºC. Bake for 12 to 14 minutes, until the eggs are set and cooked through.

## Garlic Dill Wings

**Prep time: 5 minutes | Cook time: 25 minutes | Serves 4**

| | |
|---|---|
| 900 g bone-in chicken wings, separated at joints | pepper |
| ½ teaspoon salt | ½ teaspoon onion powder |
| ½ teaspoon ground black | ½ teaspoon garlic powder |
| | 1 teaspoon dried dill |

In a large bowl, toss wings with salt, pepper, onion powder, garlic powder, and dill until evenly coated. Place wings into ungreased air fryer basket in a single layer, working in batches if needed. Adjust the temperature to 200°C and air fry for 25 minutes, shaking the basket every 7 minutes during cooking. Wings should have an internal temperature of at least 75°C and be golden brown when done. Serve warm.

## Coconut Chicken Wings with Mango Sauce

**Prep time: 15 minutes | Cook time: 20 minutes | Serves 4**

| | |
|---|---|
| 16 chicken drumettes (party wings) | coconut |
| 60 ml full-fat coconut milk | 60 g all-purpose flour |
| 1 tablespoon sriracha | Cooking oil spray |
| 1 teaspoon onion powder | 165 g mango, cut into ½-inch chunks |
| 1 teaspoon garlic powder | 15 g fresh coriander, chopped |
| Salt and freshly ground black pepper, to taste | 25 g red onion, chopped |
| 25 g shredded unsweetened | 2 garlic cloves, minced |
| | Juice of ½ lime |

Place the drumettes in a resealable plastic bag. In a small bowl, whisk the coconut milk and sriracha. Drizzle the drumettes with the sriracha–coconut milk mixture. Season the drumettes with the onion powder, garlic powder, salt, and pepper. Seal the bag. Shake it thoroughly to combine the seasonings and coat the chicken. Marinate for at least 30 minutes, preferably overnight, in the refrigerator. When the drumettes are almost done marinating, in a large bowl, stir together the shredded coconut and flour. Dip the drumettes into the coconut-flour mixture. Press the flour mixture onto the chicken with your hands. Insert the crisper plate into the basket and the basket into the unit. Preheat the unit by selecting AIR FRY, setting the temperature to 200°C, and setting the time to 3 minutes. Select START/STOP to begin. Once the unit is preheated, spray the crisper plate and the basket with cooking oil. Place the drumettes in the air fryer. It is okay to stack them. Spray the drumettes with cooking oil, being sure to cover the bottom layer. Select AIR FRY, set the temperature to 200°C, and set the time to 20 minutes. Select START/STOP to begin. After 5 minutes, remove the basket and shake it to ensure all pieces cook through. Reinsert the basket to resume cooking. Remove and shake the basket every 5 minutes, twice more, until a food thermometer inserted into the drumettes registers 75°C. 1When the cooking is complete, let the chicken cool for 5 minutes. 1While the chicken cooks and cools, make the salsa. In a small bowl, combine the mango, coriander, red onion, garlic, and lime juice. Mix well until fully combined. Serve with the wings.

## Pecan-Crusted Chicken Tenders

**Prep time: 10 minutes | Cook time: 12 minutes | Serves 4**

| | |
|---|---|
| 2 tablespoons mayonnaise | ¼ teaspoon ground black pepper |
| 1 teaspoon Dijon mustard | |
| 455 g boneless, skinless chicken tenders | 75 g chopped roasted pecans, finely ground |
| ½ teaspoon salt | |

In a small bowl, whisk mayonnaise and mustard until combined. Brush mixture onto chicken tenders on both sides, then sprinkle tenders with salt and pepper. Place pecans in a medium bowl and press each tender into pecans to coat each side. Place tenders into ungreased air fryer basket in a single layer, working in batches if needed. Adjust the temperature to (190°C and roast for 12 minutes, turning tenders halfway through cooking. Tenders will be golden brown and have an internal temperature of at least 75°C when done. Serve warm.

## Chicken Parmesan

**Prep time: 15 minutes | Cook time: 10 minutes | Serves 4**

| | |
|---|---|
| Oil, for spraying | plus 45 g shredded |
| 2 (230 g) boneless, skinless chicken breasts | 4 tablespoons unsalted butter, melted |
| 120 g Italian-style bread crumbs | 115 g marinara sauce |
| 20 g grated Parmesan cheese, | |

Preheat the air fryer to 180°C. Line the air fryer basket with parchment and spray lightly with oil. Cut each chicken breast in half through its thickness to make 4 thin cutlets. Using a meat tenderizer, pound each cutlet until it is about ¾ inch thick. On a plate, mix together the bread crumbs and grated Parmesan cheese. Lightly brush the chicken with the melted butter, then dip into the bread crumb mixture. Place the chicken in the prepared basket and spray lightly with oil. You may need to work in batches, depending on the size of your air fryer. Cook for 6 minutes. Top the chicken with the marinara and shredded Parmesan cheese, dividing evenly. Cook for another 3 to 4 minutes, or until golden brown, crispy, and the internal temperature reaches 75°C.

## Chicken Strips with Satay Sauce

**Prep time: 15 minutes | Cook time: 10 minutes | Serves 4**

| | |
|---|---|
| 4 (170 g) boneless, skinless chicken breasts, sliced into 16 (1-inch) strips | fresh ginger |
| | ½ teaspoon hot sauce |
| 1 teaspoon fine sea salt | ⅛ teaspoon stevia glycerite, or |
| 1 teaspoon paprika | 2 to 3 drops liquid stevia |
| Sauce: | For Garnish/Serving (Optional): |
| 60 g creamy almond butter (or sunflower seed butter for nut-free) | 15 g chopped coriander leaves |
| | Red pepper flakes |
| | Sea salt flakes |
| 2 tablespoons chicken broth | Thinly sliced red, orange, and |
| 1½ tablespoons coconut vinegar or unseasoned rice vinegar | yellow bell peppers |
| | Special Equipment: |
| 1 clove garlic, minced | 16 wooden or bamboo skewers, |
| 1 teaspoon peeled and minced | soaked in water for 15 minutes |

Spray the air fryer basket with avocado oil. Preheat the air fryer to 200ºC. Thread the chicken strips onto the skewers. Season on all sides with the salt and paprika. Place the chicken skewers in the air fryer basket and air fry for 5 minutes, flip, and cook for another 5 minutes, until the chicken is cooked through and the internal temperature reaches 75ºC. While the chicken skewers cook, make the sauce: In a medium-sized bowl, stir together all the sauce ingredients until well combined. Taste and adjust the sweetness and heat to your liking. Garnish the chicken with coriander, red pepper flakes, and salt flakes, if desired, and serve with sliced bell peppers, if desired. Serve the sauce on the side. Store leftovers in an airtight container in the fridge for up to 4 days or in the freezer for up to a month. Reheat in a preheated 180ºC air fryer for 3 minutes per side, or until heated through.

## Chicken, Courgette, and Spinach Salad

**Prep time: 10 minutes | Cook time: 20 minutes | Serves 4**

| | |
|---|---|
| 3 (140 g) boneless, skinless chicken breasts, cut into 1-inch cubes | 1 medium red onion, sliced |
| | 1 red bell pepper, sliced |
| 5 teaspoons extra-virgin olive oil | 1 small courgette, cut into strips |
| | 3 tablespoons freshly squeezed |
| ½ teaspoon dried thyme | lemon juice |
| | 85 g fresh baby spinach leaves |

Insert the crisper plate into the basket and the basket into the unit. Preheat the unit by selecting AIR ROAST, setting the temperature to 190ºC, and setting the time to 3 minutes. Select START/STOP to begin. In a large bowl, combine the chicken, olive oil, and thyme. Toss to coat. Transfer to a medium metal bowl that fits into the basket. Once the unit is preheated, place the bowl into the basket. Select AIR ROAST, set the temperature to 190ºC, and set the time to 20 minutes. Select START/STOP to begin. After 8 minutes, add the red onion, red bell pepper, and courgette to the bowl. Resume cooking. After about 6 minutes more, stir the chicken and vegetables. Resume cooking. When the cooking is complete, a food thermometer inserted into the chicken should register at least 75ºC. Remove the bowl from the unit and stir in the lemon juice. Put the spinach in a serving bowl and top with the chicken mixture. Toss to combine and serve immediately.

## Indian Fennel Chicken

**Prep time: 30 minutes | Cook time: 15 minutes | Serves 4**

| | |
|---|---|
| 450 g boneless, skinless chicken thighs, cut crosswise into thirds | 1 teaspoon ground fennel |
| | 1 teaspoon garam masala |
| 1 yellow onion, cut into 1½-inch-thick slices | 1 teaspoon ground turmeric |
| | 1 teaspoon kosher salt |
| 1 tablespoon coconut oil, melted | ½ to 1 teaspoon cayenne pepper |
| | Vegetable oil spray |
| 2 teaspoons minced fresh ginger | 2 teaspoons fresh lemon juice |
| 2 teaspoons minced garlic | 5 g chopped fresh coriander or |
| 1 teaspoon smoked paprika | parsley |

Use a fork to pierce the chicken all over to allow the marinade to penetrate better. In a large bowl, combine the onion, coconut oil, ginger, garlic, paprika, fennel, garam masala, turmeric, salt, and cayenne. Add the chicken, toss to combine, and marinate at room temperature for 30 minutes, or cover and refrigerate for up to 24 hours. Place the chicken and onion in the air fryer basket. (Discard remaining marinade.) Spray with some vegetable oil spray. Set the air fryer to 180ºC for 15 minutes. Halfway through the cooking time, remove the basket, spray the chicken and onion with more vegetable oil spray, and toss gently to coat. At the end of the cooking time, use a meat thermometer to ensure the chicken has reached an internal temperature of 75ºC. Transfer the chicken and onion to a serving platter. Sprinkle with the lemon juice and coriander and serve.

## Greek Chicken Souvlaki

**Prep time: 30 minutes | Cook time: 15 minutes | Serves 3 to 4**

| | |
|---|---|
| Chicken: | Vegetable oil spray |
| Grated zest and juice of 1 lemon | For Serving: |
| | Warm pita bread or hot cooked rice |
| 2 tablespoons extra-virgin olive oil | |
| | Sliced ripe tomatoes |
| 1 tablespoon Greek souvlaki seasoning | Sliced cucumbers |
| | Thinly sliced red onion |
| 450 g boneless, skinless chicken breast, cut into 2-inch chunks | Kalamata olives |
| | Tzatziki |

For the chicken: In a small bowl, combine the lemon zest, lemon juice, olive oil, and souvlaki seasoning. Place the chicken in a gallon-size resealable plastic bag. Pour the marinade over chicken. Seal bag and massage to coat. Place the bag in a large bowl and marinate for 30 minutes, or cover and refrigerate up to 24 hours, turning the bag occasionally. Place the chicken a single layer in the air fryer basket. Set the air fryer to 180ºC for 10 minutes, turning the chicken and spraying with a little vegetable oil spray halfway through the cooking time. Increase the air fryer temperature to 200ºC for 5 minutes to allow the chicken to crisp and brown a little. Transfer the chicken to a serving platter and serve with pita bread or rice, tomatoes, cucumbers, onion, olives and tzatziki.

## Wild Rice and Kale Stuffed Chicken Thighs

**Prep time: 10 minutes | Cook time: 22 minutes | Serves 4**

| | |
|---|---|
| 4 boneless, skinless chicken thighs | 1 teaspoon salt |
| 250 g cooked wild rice | Juice of 1 lemon |
| 35 g chopped kale | 100 g crumbled feta |
| 2 garlic cloves, minced | Olive oil cooking spray |
| | 1 tablespoon olive oi |

Preheat the air fryer to 190°C. Place the chicken thighs between two pieces of plastic wrap, and using a meat mallet or a rolling pin, pound them out to about ¼-inch thick. In a medium bowl, combine the rice, kale, garlic, salt, and lemon juice and mix well. Place a quarter of the rice mixture into the middle of each chicken thigh, then sprinkle 2 tablespoons of feta over the filling. Spray the air fryer basket with olive oil cooking spray. Fold the sides of the chicken thigh over the filling, and then gently place each of them seam-side down into the air fryer basket. Brush each stuffed chicken thigh with olive oil. Roast the stuffed chicken thighs for 12 minutes, then turn them over and cook for an additional 10 minutes, or until the internal temperature reaches 75°C.

## Honey-Glazed Chicken Thighs

**Prep time: 5 minutes | Cook time: 14 minutes | Serves 4**

| | |
|---|---|
| Oil, for spraying | 1 tablespoon balsamic vinegar |
| 4 boneless, skinless chicken thighs, fat trimmed | 2 teaspoons honey |
| 3 tablespoons soy sauce | 2 teaspoons minced garlic |
| | 1 teaspoon ground ginger |

Preheat the air fryer to 200°C. Line the air fryer basket with parchment and spray lightly with oil. Place the chicken in the prepared basket. Cook for 7 minutes, flip, and cook for another 7 minutes, or until the internal temperature reaches 75°C and the juices run clear. In a small saucepan, combine the soy sauce, balsamic vinegar, honey, garlic, and ginger and cook over low heat for 1 to 2 minutes, until warmed through. Transfer the chicken to a serving plate and drizzle with the sauce just before serving.

## Air Fried Chicken Potatoes with Sun-Dried Tomato

**Prep time: 15 minutes | Cook time: 25 minutes | Serves 2**

| | |
|---|---|
| 2 teaspoons minced fresh oregano, divided | 15 g oil-packed sun-dried tomatoes, patted dry and chopped |
| 2 teaspoons minced fresh thyme, divided | 1½ tablespoons red wine vinegar |
| 2 teaspoons extra-virgin olive oil, plus extra as needed | 1 tablespoon capers, rinsed and minced |
| 450 g fingerling potatoes, unpeeled | 1 small shallot, minced |
| 2 (340 g) bone-in split chicken breasts, trimmed | Salt and ground black pepper, to taste |
| 1 garlic clove, minced | |

Preheat the air fryer to 180°C. Combine 1 teaspoon of oregano, 1

teaspoon of thyme, ¼ teaspoon of salt, ¼ teaspoon of ground black pepper, 1 teaspoons of olive oil in a large bowl. Add the potatoes and toss to coat well. Combine the chicken with remaining thyme, oregano, and olive oil. Sprinkle with garlic, salt, and pepper. Toss to coat well. Place the potatoes in the preheated air fryer, then arrange the chicken on top of the potatoes. Air fry for 25 minutes or until the internal temperature of the chicken reaches at least 75°C and the potatoes are wilted. Flip the chicken and potatoes halfway through. Meanwhile, combine the sun-dried tomatoes, vinegar, capers, and shallot in a separate large bowl. Sprinkle with salt and ground black pepper. Toss to mix well. Remove the chicken and potatoes from the air fryer and allow to cool for 10 minutes. Serve with the sun-dried tomato mix.

## Juicy Paprika Chicken Breast

**Prep time: 5 minutes | Cook time: 30 minutes | Serves 4**

| | |
|---|---|
| Oil, for spraying | 1 tablespoon packed light brown sugar |
| 4 (170 g) boneless, skinless chicken breasts | ½ teaspoon cayenne pepper |
| 1 tablespoon olive oil | ½ teaspoon onion powder |
| 1 tablespoon paprika | ½ teaspoon granulated garlic |

Line the air fryer basket with parchment and spray lightly with oil. Brush the chicken with the olive oil. In a small bowl, mix together the paprika, brown sugar, cayenne pepper, onion powder, and garlic and sprinkle it over the chicken. Place the chicken in the prepared basket. You may need to work in batches, depending on the size of your air fryer. Air fry at 180°C for 15 minutes, flip, and cook for another 15 minutes, or until the internal temperature reaches 75°C. Serve immediately.

## Hawaiian Chicken Bites

**Prep time: 1 hour 15 minutes | Cook time: 15 minutes | Serves 4**

| | |
|---|---|
| 120 ml pineapple juice | 110 g brown sugar |
| 2 tablespoons apple cider vinegar | 2 tablespoons sherry |
| ½ tablespoon minced ginger | 120 ml soy sauce |
| 120 g ketchup | 4 chicken breasts, cubed |
| 2 garlic cloves, minced | Cooking spray |

Combine the pineapple juice, cider vinegar, ginger, ketchup, garlic, and sugar in a saucepan. Stir to mix well. Heat over low heat for 5 minutes or until thickened. Fold in the sherry and soy sauce. Dunk the chicken cubes in the mixture. Press to submerge. Wrap the bowl in plastic and refrigerate to marinate for at least an hour. Preheat the air fryer to 180°C. Spritz the air fryer basket with cooking spray. Remove the chicken cubes from the marinade. Shake the excess off and put in the preheated air fryer. Spritz with cooking spray. Air fry for 15 minutes or until the chicken cubes are glazed and well browned. Shake the basket at least three times during the frying. Serve immediately.

## Cracked-Pepper Chicken Wings

**Prep time: 15 minutes | Cook time: 20 minutes | Serves 4**

| | |
|---|---|
| 450 g chicken wings | ½ teaspoon garlic powder |
| 3 tablespoons vegetable oil | ½ teaspoon kosher salt |
| 60 g all-purpose flour | 1½ teaspoons freshly cracked |
| ½ teaspoon smoked paprika | black pepper |

Place the chicken wings in a large bowl. Drizzle the vegetable oil over wings and toss to coat. In a separate bowl, whisk together the flour, paprika, garlic powder, salt, and pepper until combined. Dredge the wings in the flour mixture one at a time, coating them well, and place in the air fryer basket. Set the air fryer to 200°C for 20 minutes, turning the wings halfway through the cooking time, until the breading is browned and crunchy.

## Broccoli and Cheese Stuffed Chicken

**Prep time: 15 minutes | Cook time: 20 minutes | Serves 4**

| | |
|---|---|
| 60 g cream cheese, softened | chicken breasts |
| 70 g chopped fresh broccoli, steamed | 2 tablespoons mayonnaise |
| 120 g shredded sharp Cheddar cheese | ¼ teaspoon salt |
| 4 (170 g) boneless, skinless | ¼ teaspoon garlic powder |
| | ⅛ teaspoon ground black pepper |

In a medium bowl, combine cream cheese, broccoli, and Cheddar. Cut a 4-inch pocket into each chicken breast. Evenly divide mixture between chicken breasts; stuff the pocket of each chicken breast with the mixture. Spread ¼ tablespoon mayonnaise per side of each chicken breast, then sprinkle both sides of breasts with salt, garlic powder, and pepper. Place stuffed chicken breasts into ungreased air fryer basket so that the open seams face up. Adjust the temperature to 180°C and air fry for 20 minutes, turning chicken halfway through cooking. When done, chicken will be golden and have an internal temperature of at least 75°C. Serve warm.

## Broccoli Cheese Chicken

**Prep time: 15 minutes | Cook time: 25 minutes | Serves 4**

| | |
|---|---|
| 1 tablespoon avocado oil | additional for seasoning, divided |
| 15 g chopped onion | |
| 35 g finely chopped broccoli | ¼ freshly ground black pepper, plus additional for seasoning, divided |
| 115 g cream cheese, at room temperature | |
| 60 g Cheddar cheese, shredded | 900 g boneless, skinless chicken breasts |
| 1 teaspoon garlic powder | |
| ½ teaspoon sea salt, plus | 1 teaspoon smoked paprika |

Heat a medium skillet over medium-high heat and pour in the avocado oil. Add the onion and broccoli and cook, stirring occasionally, for 5 to 8 minutes, until the onion is tender. Transfer to a large bowl and stir in the cream cheese, Cheddar cheese, and garlic powder, and season to taste with salt and pepper. Hold a sharp knife parallel to the chicken breast and cut a long pocket into one side. Stuff the chicken pockets with the broccoli mixture,

using toothpicks to secure the pockets around the filling. In a small dish, combine the paprika, ½ teaspoon salt, and ¼ teaspoon pepper. Sprinkle this over the outside of the chicken. Set the air fryer to 200°C. Place the chicken in a single layer in the air fryer basket, cooking in batches if necessary, and cook for 14 to 16 minutes, until an instant-read thermometer reads 70°C. Place the chicken on a plate and tent a piece of aluminum foil over the chicken. Allow to rest for 5 to 10 minutes before serving.

## Crispy Dill Chicken Strips

**Prep time: 30 minutes | Cook time: 10 minutes | Serves 4**

| | |
|---|---|
| 2 whole boneless, skinless chicken breasts (about 450 g each), halved lengthwise | 1 tablespoon dried dill weed |
| | 1 tablespoon garlic powder |
| | 1 large egg, beaten |
| 230 ml Italian dressing | 1 to 2 tablespoons oil |
| 110 g finely crushed crisps | |

In a large resealable bag, combine the chicken and Italian dressing. Seal the bag and refrigerate to marinate at least 1 hour. In a shallow dish, stir together the potato chips, dill, and garlic powder. Place the beaten egg in a second shallow dish. Remove the chicken from the marinade. Roll the chicken pieces in the egg and the crisp mixture, coating thoroughly. Preheat the air fryer to 170°C. Line the air fryer basket with parchment paper. Place the coated chicken on the parchment and spritz with oil. Cook for 5 minutes. Flip the chicken, spritz it with oil, and cook for 5 minutes more until the outsides are crispy and the insides are no longer pink.

## Sweet Chili Spiced Chicken

**Prep time: 10 minutes | Cook time: 43 minutes | Serves 4**

| | |
|---|---|
| Spice Rub: | kosher salt |
| 2 tablespoons brown sugar | 2 teaspoons coarsely ground black pepper |
| 2 tablespoons paprika | |
| 1 teaspoon dry mustard powder | 1 tablespoon vegetable oil |
| 1 teaspoon chili powder | 1 (1.6 kg) chicken, cut into 8 |
| 2 tablespoons coarse sea salt or | pieces |

Prepare the spice rub by combining the brown sugar, paprika, mustard powder, chili powder, salt and pepper. Rub the oil all over the chicken pieces and then rub the spice mix onto the chicken, covering completely. This is done very easily in a zipper sealable bag. You can do this ahead of time and let the chicken marinate in the refrigerator, or just proceed with cooking right away. Preheat the air fryer to 190°C. Air fry the chicken in two batches. Place the two chicken thighs and two drumsticks into the air fryer basket. Air fry at 190°C for 10 minutes. Then, gently turn the chicken pieces over and air fry for another 10 minutes. Remove the chicken pieces and let them rest on a plate while you cook the chicken breasts. Air fry the chicken breasts, skin side down for 8 minutes. Turn the chicken breasts over and air fry for another 12 minutes. Lower the temperature of the air fryer to 170°C. Place the first batch of chicken on top of the second batch already in the basket and air fry for a final 3 minutes. Let the chicken rest for 5 minutes and serve warm with some mashed potatoes and a green salad or vegetables.

## Chicken with Bacon and Tomato

**Prep time: 25 minutes | Cook time: 10 minutes | Serves 4**

4 medium-sized skin-on chicken drumsticks
1½ teaspoons herbs de Provence
Salt and pepper, to taste
1 tablespoon rice vinegar
2 tablespoons olive oil
2 garlic cloves, crushed
340 g crushed canned tomatoes
1 small-size leek, thinly sliced
2 slices smoked bacon, chopped

Sprinkle the chicken drumsticks with herbs de Provence, salt and pepper; then, drizzle them with rice vinegar and olive oil. Cook in the baking pan at 180°C for 8 to 10 minutes. Pause the air fryer; stir in the remaining ingredients and continue to cook for 15 minutes longer; make sure to check them periodically. Bon appétit!

## Curried Orange Honey Chicken

**Prep time: 10 minutes | Cook time: 16 to 19 minutes | Serves 4**

340 g boneless, skinless chicken thighs, cut into 1-inch pieces
1 yellow bell pepper, cut into 1½-inch pieces
1 small red onion, sliced
Olive oil for misting
60 ml chicken stock
2 tablespoons honey
60 ml orange juice
1 tablespoon cornflour
2 to 3 teaspoons curry powder

Preheat the air fryer to 190°C. Put the chicken thighs, pepper, and red onion in the air fryer basket and mist with olive oil. Roast for 12 to 14 minutes or until the chicken is cooked to 75°C, shaking the basket halfway through cooking time. Remove the chicken and vegetables from the air fryer basket and set aside. In a metal bowl, combine the stock, honey, orange juice, cornflour, and curry powder, and mix well. Add the chicken and vegetables, stir, and put the bowl in the basket. Return the basket to the air fryer and roast for 2 minutes. Remove and stir, then roast for 2 to 3 minutes or until the sauce is thickened and bubbly. Serve warm.

## Herbed Turkey Breast with Simple Dijon Sauce

**Prep time: 5 minutes | Cook time: 30 minutes | Serves 4**

1 teaspoon chopped fresh sage
1 teaspoon chopped fresh tarragon
1 teaspoon chopped fresh thyme leaves
1 teaspoon chopped fresh rosemary leaves
1½ teaspoons sea salt
1 teaspoon ground black pepper
1 (900 g) turkey breast
3 tablespoons Dijon mustard
3 tablespoons butter, melted
Cooking spray

Preheat the air fryer to 200°C. Spritz the air fryer basket with cooking spray. Combine the herbs, salt, and black pepper in a small bowl. Stir to mix well. Set aside. Combine the Dijon mustard and butter in a separate bowl. Stir to mix well. Rub the turkey with the herb mixture on a clean work surface, then brush the turkey with

Dijon mixture. Arrange the turkey in the preheated air fryer basket. Air fry for 30 minutes or until an instant-read thermometer inserted in the thickest part of the turkey breast reaches at least 75°C. Transfer the cooked turkey breast on a large plate and slice to serve.

## Coriander Lime Chicken Thighs

**Prep time: 15 minutes | Cook time: 22 minutes | Serves 4**

4 bone-in, skin-on chicken thighs
1 teaspoon baking powder
½ teaspoon garlic powder
2 teaspoons chili powder
1 teaspoon cumin
2 medium limes
5 g chopped fresh coriander

Pat chicken thighs dry and sprinkle with baking powder. In a small bowl, mix garlic powder, chili powder, and cumin and sprinkle evenly over thighs, gently rubbing on and under chicken skin. Cut one lime in half and squeeze juice over thighs. Place chicken into the air fryer basket. Adjust the temperature to 190°C and roast for 22 minutes. Cut other lime into four wedges for serving and garnish cooked chicken with wedges and coriander.

## Chicken Pesto Pizzas

**Prep time: 10 minutes | Cook time: 12 minutes | Serves 4**

450 g chicken mince thighs
¼ teaspoon salt
⅛ teaspoon ground black pepper
20 g basil pesto
225 g shredded Mozzarella cheese
4 grape tomatoes, sliced

Cut four squares of parchment paper to fit into your air fryer basket. Place chicken mince in a large bowl and mix with salt and pepper. Divide mixture into four equal sections. Wet your hands with water to prevent sticking, then press each section into a 6-inch circle onto a piece of ungreased parchment. Place each chicken crust into air fryer basket, working in batches if needed. Adjust the temperature to 180°C and air fry for 10 minutes, turning crusts halfway through cooking. Spread 1 tablespoon pesto across the top of each crust, then sprinkle with ¼ of the Mozzarella and top with 1 sliced tomato. Continue cooking at 180°C for 2 minutes. Cheese will be melted and brown when done. Serve warm.

## Chicken Legs with Leeks

**Prep time: 30 minutes | Cook time: 18 minutes | Serves 6**

2 leeks, sliced
2 large-sized tomatoes, chopped
3 cloves garlic, minced
½ teaspoon dried oregano
6 chicken legs, boneless and
skinless
½ teaspoon smoked cayenne pepper
2 tablespoons olive oil
A freshly ground nutmeg

In a mixing dish, thoroughly combine all ingredients, minus the leeks. Place in the refrigerator and let it marinate overnight. Lay the leeks onto the bottom of the air fryer basket. Top with the chicken legs. Roast chicken legs at (190°C for 18 minutes, turning halfway through. Serve with hoisin sauce.

## Chicken Patties

**Prep time: 15 minutes | Cook time: 12 minutes | Serves 4**

| | |
|---|---|
| 450 g chicken thigh mince | ½ teaspoon garlic powder |
| 110 g shredded Mozzarella cheese | ¼ teaspoon onion powder |
| 1 teaspoon dried parsley | 1 large egg |
| | 60 g pork rinds, finely ground |

In a large bowl, mix chicken mince, Mozzarella, parsley, garlic powder, and onion powder. Form into four patties. Place patties in the freezer for 15 to 20 minutes until they begin to firm up. Whisk egg in a medium bowl. Place the ground pork rinds into a large bowl. Dip each chicken patty into the egg and then press into pork rinds to fully coat. Place patties into the air fryer basket. Adjust the temperature to 180°C and air fry for 12 minutes. Patties will be firm and cooked to an internal temperature of 75°C when done. Serve immediately.

## One-Dish Chicken and Rice

**Prep time: 10 minutes | Cook time: 40 minutes | Serves 4**

| | |
|---|---|
| 190 g long-grain white rice, rinsed and drained | 3 cloves garlic, minced |
| 120 g cut frozen green beans (do not thaw) | 1 tablespoon toasted sesame oil |
| 1 tablespoon minced fresh ginger | 1 teaspoon kosher salt |
| | 1 teaspoon black pepper |
| | 450 g chicken wings, preferably drumettes |

In a baking pan, combine the rice, green beans, ginger, garlic, sesame oil, salt, and pepper. Stir to combine. Place the chicken wings on top of the rice mixture. Cover the pan with foil. Make a long slash in the foil to allow the pan to vent steam. Place the pan in the air fryer basket. Set the air fryer to (190°C for 30 minutes. Remove the foil. Set the air fryer to 200°C for 10 minutes, or until the wings have browned and rendered fat into the rice and vegetables, turning the wings halfway through the cooking time.

## Butter and Bacon Chicken

**Prep time: 10 minutes | Cook time: 65 minutes | Serves 6**

| | |
|---|---|
| 1 (1.8 kg) whole chicken | 1 teaspoon salt |
| 2 tablespoons salted butter, softened | ½ teaspoon ground black pepper |
| 1 teaspoon dried thyme | 6 slices sugar-free bacon |
| ½ teaspoon garlic powder | |

Pat chicken dry with a paper towel, then rub with butter on all sides. Sprinkle thyme, garlic powder, salt, and pepper over chicken. Place chicken into ungreased air fryer basket, breast side up. Lay strips of bacon over chicken and secure with toothpicks. Adjust the temperature to 180°C and air fry for 65 minutes. Halfway through cooking, remove and set aside bacon and flip chicken over. Chicken will be done when the skin is golden and crispy and the internal temperature is at least 75°C. Serve warm with bacon.

## Thai Curry Meatballs

**Prep time: 10 minutes | Cook time: 10 minutes | Serves 4**

| | |
|---|---|
| 450 g chicken mince | 1 tablespoon fish sauce |
| 15 g chopped fresh coriander | 2 garlic cloves, minced |
| 1 teaspoon chopped fresh mint | 2 teaspoons minced fresh ginger |
| 1 tablespoon fresh lime juice | ½ teaspoon kosher salt |
| 1 tablespoon Thai red, green, or yellow curry paste | ½ teaspoon black pepper |
| | ¼ teaspoon red pepper flakes |

Preheat the air fryer to 200°C. In a large bowl, gently mix the chicken mince, coriander, mint, lime juice, curry paste, fish sauce, garlic, ginger, salt, black pepper, and red pepper flakes until thoroughly combined. Form the mixture into 16 meatballs. Place the meatballs in a single layer in the air fryer basket. Air fry for 10 minutes, turning the meatballs halfway through the cooking time. Use a meat thermometer to ensure the meatballs have reached an internal temperature of 75°C. Serve immediately.

## Apricot-Glazed Turkey Tenderloin

**Prep time: 20 minutes | Cook time: 30 minutes | Serves 4**

| | |
|---|---|
| Olive oil | mustard |
| 80 g sugar-free apricot preserves | 680 g turkey breast tenderloin |
| ½ tablespoon spicy brown | Salt and freshly ground black pepper, to taste |

Spray the air fryer basket lightly with olive oil. In a small bowl, combine the apricot preserves and mustard to make a paste. Season the turkey with salt and pepper. Spread the apricot paste all over the turkey. Place the turkey in the air fryer basket and lightly spray with olive oil. Air fry at 190°C for 15 minutes. Flip the turkey over and lightly spray with olive oil. Air fry until the internal temperature reaches at least 80°C, an additional 10 to 15 minutes. Let the turkey rest for 10 minutes before slicing and serving.

## Nice Goulash

**Prep time: 5 minutes | Cook time: 17 minutes | Serves 2**

| | |
|---|---|
| 2 red bell peppers, chopped | Salt and ground black pepper, to taste |
| 450 g chicken mince | Cooking spray |
| 2 medium tomatoes, diced | |
| 120 ml chicken broth | |

Preheat the air fryer to 185°C. Spritz a baking pan with cooking spray. Set the bell pepper in the baking pan and put in the air fry to broil for 5 minutes or until the bell pepper is tender. Shake the basket halfway through. Add the chicken mince and diced tomatoes in the baking pan and stir to mix well. Broil for 6 more minutes or until the chicken is lightly browned. Pour the chicken broth over and sprinkle with salt and ground black pepper. Stir to mix well. Broil for an additional 6 minutes. Serve immediately.

## Lemon Thyme Roasted Chicken

**Prep time: 10 minutes | Cook time: 60 minutes | Serves 6**

| | |
|---|---|
| 2 tablespoons baking powder | 80 ml avocado oil |
| 1 teaspoon smoked paprika | 120 ml Buffalo hot sauce, such |
| Sea salt and freshly ground | as Frank's RedHot |
| black pepper, to taste | 4 tablespoons unsalted butter |
| 900 g chicken wings or chicken | 2 tablespoons apple cider |
| drumettes | vinegar |
| Avocado oil spray | 1 teaspoon minced garlic |

In a large bowl, stir together the baking powder, smoked paprika, and salt and pepper to taste. Add the chicken wings and toss to coat. Set the air fryer to 200ºC. Spray the wings with oil. Place the wings in the basket in a single layer, working in batches, and air fry for 20 to 25 minutes. Check with an instant-read thermometer and remove when they reach 70ºC. Let rest until they reach 75ºC. While the wings are cooking, whisk together the avocado oil, hot sauce, butter, vinegar, and garlic in a small saucepan over medium-low heat until warm. When the wings are done cooking, toss them with the Buffalo sauce. Serve warm.

## Teriyaki Chicken Legs

**Prep time: 12 minutes | Cook time: 18 to 20 minutes | Serves 2**

| | |
|---|---|
| 4 tablespoons teriyaki sauce | 4 chicken legs |
| 1 tablespoon orange juice | Cooking spray |
| 1 teaspoon smoked paprika | |

Mix together the teriyaki sauce, orange juice, and smoked paprika. Brush on all sides of chicken legs. Spray the air fryer basket with nonstick cooking spray and place chicken in basket. Air fry at 180ºC for 6 minutes. Turn and baste with sauce. Cook for 6 more minutes, turn and baste. Cook for 6 to 8 minutes more, until juices run clear when chicken is pierced with a fork.

## Simply Terrific Turkey Meatballs

**Prep time: 10 minutes | Cook time: 7 to 10 minutes | Serves 4**

| | |
|---|---|
| 1 red bell pepper, seeded and | 1 egg, lightly beaten |
| coarsely chopped | 45 g grated Parmesan cheese |
| 2 cloves garlic, coarsely | 1 teaspoon salt |
| chopped | ½ teaspoon freshly ground |
| 15 g chopped fresh parsley | black pepper |
| 680 g 85% lean turkey mince | |

Preheat the air fryer to 200ºC. In a food processor fitted with a metal blade, combine the bell pepper, garlic, and parsley. Pulse until finely chopped. Transfer the vegetables to a large mixing bowl. Add the turkey, egg, Parmesan, salt, and black pepper. Mix gently until thoroughly combined. Shape the mixture into 1¼-inch meatballs. Working in batches if necessary, arrange the meatballs in a single layer in the air fryer basket; coat lightly with olive oil spray. Pausing halfway through the cooking time to shake the basket, air fry for 7 to 10 minutes, until lightly browned and a thermometer inserted into the centre of a meatball registers 75ºC.

## Italian Flavour Chicken Breasts with Roma Tomatoes

**Prep time: 10 minutes | Cook time: 60 minutes | Serves 8**

| | |
|---|---|
| 1.4 kg chicken breasts, bone-in | ½ teaspoon salt |
| 1 teaspoon minced fresh basil | ½ teaspoon freshly ground |
| 1 teaspoon minced fresh | black pepper |
| rosemary | 4 medium Roma tomatoes, |
| 2 tablespoons minced fresh | halved |
| parsley | Cooking spray |
| 1 teaspoon cayenne pepper | |

Preheat the air fryer to 190ºC. Spritz the air fryer basket with cooking spray. Combine all the ingredients, except for the chicken breasts and tomatoes, in a large bowl. Stir to mix well. Dunk the chicken breasts in the mixture and press to coat well. Transfer the chicken breasts in the preheated air fryer. You may need to work in batches to avoid overcrowding. Air fry for 25 minutes or until the internal temperature of the thickest part of the breasts reaches at least 75ºC. Flip the breasts halfway through the cooking time. Remove the cooked chicken breasts from the basket and adjust the temperature to 180ºC. Place the tomatoes in the air fryer and spritz with cooking spray. Sprinkle with a touch of salt and cook for 10 minutes or until tender. Shake the basket halfway through the cooking time. Serve the tomatoes with chicken breasts on a large serving plate.

## Stuffed Chicken Florentine

**Prep time: 10 minutes | Cook time: 20 minutes | Serves 4**

| | |
|---|---|
| 3 tablespoons pine nuts | Salt and freshly ground black |
| 40 g frozen spinach, thawed | pepper, to taste |
| and squeezed dry | 4 small boneless, skinless |
| 75 g ricotta cheese | chicken breast halves (about |
| 2 tablespoons grated Parmesan | 680 g) |
| cheese | 8 slices bacon |
| 3 cloves garlic, minced | |

Place the pine nuts in a small pan and set in the air fryer basket. Set the air fryer to 200ºC and air fry for 2 to 3 minutes until toasted. Remove the pine nuts to a mixing bowl and continue preheating the air fryer. In a large bowl, combine the spinach, ricotta, Parmesan, and garlic. Season to taste with salt and pepper and stir well until thoroughly combined. Using a sharp knife, cut into the chicken breasts, slicing them across and opening them up like a book, but be careful not to cut them all the way through. Sprinkle the chicken with salt and pepper. Spoon equal amounts of the spinach mixture into the chicken, then fold the top of the chicken breast back over the top of the stuffing. Wrap each chicken breast with 2 slices of bacon. Working in batches if necessary, air fry the chicken for 18 to 20 minutes until the bacon is crisp and a thermometer inserted into the thickest part of the chicken registers 75ºC.

## Harissa-Rubbed Chicken

**Prep time: 30 minutes | Cook time: 21 minutes | Serves 4**

| | |
|---|---|
| Harissa: | 1 teaspoon kosher salt |
| 120 ml olive oil | ½ to 1 teaspoon cayenne pepper |
| 6 cloves garlic, minced | Chickens: |
| 2 tablespoons smoked paprika | 120 g yogurt |
| 1 tablespoon ground coriander | 2 small chickens, any |
| 1 tablespoon ground cumin | giblets removed, split in half |
| 1 teaspoon ground caraway | lengthwise |

For the harissa: In a medium microwave-safe bowl, combine the oil, garlic, paprika, coriander, cumin, caraway, salt, and cayenne. Microwave on high for 1 minute, stirring halfway through the cooking time. (You can also heat this on the stovetop until the oil is hot and bubbling. Or, if you must use your air fryer for everything, cook it in the air fryer at 180ºC for 5 to 6 minutes, or until the paste is heated through.) For the chicken: In a small bowl, combine 1 to 2 tablespoons harissa and the yogurt. Whisk until well combined. Place the chicken halves in a resealable plastic bag and pour the marinade over. Seal the bag and massage until all of the pieces are thoroughly coated. Marinate at room temperature for 30 minutes or in the refrigerator for up to 24 hours. Arrange the hen halves in a single layer in the air fryer basket. (If you have a smaller air fryer, you may have to cook this in two batches.) Set the air fryer to 200ºC for 20 minutes. Use a meat thermometer to ensure the chickens have reached an internal temperature of 75ºC.

## Easy Cajun Chicken Drumsticks

**Prep time: 5 minutes | Cook time: 40 minutes | Serves 5**

| | |
|---|---|
| 1 tablespoon olive oil | seasoning |
| 10 chicken drumsticks | Salt and ground black pepper, |
| 1½ tablespoons Cajun | to taste |

Preheat the air fryer to 200ºC. Grease the air fryer basket with olive oil. On a clean work surface, rub the chicken drumsticks with Cajun seasoning, salt, and ground black pepper. Arrange the seasoned chicken drumsticks in a single layer in the air fryer. You need to work in batches to avoid overcrowding. Air fry for 18 minutes or until lightly browned. Flip the drumsticks halfway through. Remove the chicken drumsticks from the air fryer. Serve immediately.

## Chicken Wings with Piri Piri Sauce

**Prep time: 30 minutes | Cook time: 30 minutes | Serves 6**

| | |
|---|---|
| 12 chicken wings | and chopped |
| 45 g butter, melted | 1 tablespoon pimiento, seeded |
| 1 teaspoon onion powder | and minced |
| ½ teaspoon cumin powder | 1 garlic clove, chopped |
| 1 teaspoon garlic paste | 2 tablespoons fresh lemon juice |
| Sauce: | ⅓ teaspoon sea salt |
| 60 g piri piri peppers, stemmed | ½ teaspoon tarragon |

Steam the chicken wings using a steamer basket that is placed over a saucepan with boiling water; reduce the heat. Now, steam the wings for 10 minutes over a moderate heat. Toss the wings with butter, onion powder, cumin powder, and garlic paste. Let the chicken wings cool to room temperature. Then, refrigerate them for 45 to 50 minutes. Roast in the preheated air fryer at 170ºC for 25 to 30 minutes; make sure to flip them halfway through. While the chicken wings are cooking, prepare the sauce by mixing all of the sauce ingredients in a food processor. Toss the wings with prepared Piri Piri Sauce and serve.

## Garlic Soy Chicken Thighs

**Prep time: 10 minutes | Cook time: 30 minutes |**

**Serves 1 to 2**

| | |
|---|---|
| 2 tablespoons chicken stock | 2 large spring onions, cut into |
| 2 tablespoons reduced-sodium | 2- to 3-inch batons, plus more, |
| soy sauce | thinly sliced, for garnish |
| 1½ tablespoons sugar | 2 bone-in, skin-on chicken |
| 4 garlic cloves, smashed and | thighs (198 to 225 g each) |
| peeled | |

Preheat the air fryer to 190ºC. In a metal cake pan, combine the chicken stock, soy sauce, and sugar and stir until the sugar dissolves. Add the garlic cloves, spring onions, and chicken thighs, turning the thighs to coat them in the marinade, then resting them skin-side up. Place the pan in the air fryer and bake, flipping the thighs every 5 minutes after the first 10 minutes, until the chicken is cooked through and the marinade is reduced to a sticky glaze over the chicken, about 30 minutes. Remove the pan from the air fryer and serve the chicken thighs warm, with any remaining glaze spooned over top and sprinkled with more sliced spring onions.

## Jerk Chicken Thighs

**Prep time: 30 minutes | Cook time: 15 to 20 minutes**

**| Serves 6**

| | |
|---|---|
| 2 teaspoons ground coriander | ½ teaspoon ground cinnamon |
| 1 teaspoon ground allspice | ½ teaspoon ground nutmeg |
| 1 teaspoon cayenne pepper | 900 g boneless chicken thighs, |
| 1 teaspoon ground ginger | skin on |
| 1 teaspoon salt | 2 tablespoons olive oil |
| 1 teaspoon dried thyme | |

In a small bowl, combine the coriander, allspice, cayenne, ginger, salt, thyme, cinnamon, and nutmeg. Stir until thoroughly combined. Place the chicken in a baking dish and use paper towels to pat dry. Thoroughly coat both sides of the chicken with the spice mixture. Cover and refrigerate for at least 2 hours, preferably overnight. Preheat the air fryer to 180ºC. Working in batches if necessary, arrange the chicken in a single layer in the air fryer basket and lightly coat with the olive oil. Pausing halfway through the cooking time to flip the chicken, air fry for 15 to 20 minutes, until a thermometer inserted into the thickest part registers 75ºC.

# Chapter 4 Beef, Pork, and Lamb

## Chorizo and Beef Burger

**Prep time: 10 minutes | Cook time: 15 minutes | Serves 4**

340 g 80/20 beef mince
110 g Mexican-style chorizo
crumb
60 ml chopped onion
5 slices pickled jalapeños,

chopped
2 teaspoons chili powder
1 teaspoon minced garlic
¼ teaspoon cumin

In a large bowl, mix all ingredients. Divide the mixture into four sections and form them into burger patties. Place burger patties into the air fryer basket, working in batches if necessary. Adjust the temperature to 190ºC and air fry for 15 minutes. Flip the patties halfway through the cooking time. Serve warm.

## Cinnamon-Beef Kofta

**Prep time: 10 minutes | Cook time: 13 minutes per batch | Makes 12 koftas**

680 g lean beef mince
1 teaspoon onion granules
¾ teaspoon ground cinnamon
¾ teaspoon ground dried
turmeric
1 teaspoon ground cumin

¾ teaspoon salt
¼ teaspoon cayenne
12 (3½- to 4-inch-long)
cinnamon sticks
Cooking spray

Preheat the air fryer to 190ºC. Spritz the air fryer basket with cooking spray. Combine all the ingredients, except for the cinnamon sticks, in a large bowl. Toss to mix well. Divide and shape the mixture into 12 balls, then wrap each ball around each cinnamon stick and leave a quarter of the length uncovered. Arrange the beef-cinnamon sticks in the preheated air fryer and spritz with cooking spray. Work in batches to avoid overcrowding. Air fry for 13 minutes or until the beef is browned. Flip the sticks halfway through. Serve immediately.

## Green Pepper Cheeseburgers

**Prep time: 5 minutes | Cook time: 30 minutes | Serves 4**

2 green peppers
680 g 85% lean beef mince
1 clove garlic, minced
1 teaspoon salt
½ teaspoon freshly ground

black pepper
4 slices Cheddar cheese (about
85 g)
4 large lettuce leaves

Preheat the air fryer to 200ºC. Arrange the peppers in the basket of the air fryer. Pausing halfway through the cooking time to turn the peppers, air fry for 20 minutes, or until they are softened and beginning to char. Transfer the peppers to a large bowl and cover with a plate. When cool enough to handle, peel off the skin, remove the seeds and stems, and slice into strips. Set aside. Meanwhile, in a large bowl, combine the beef with the garlic, salt, and pepper. Shape the beef into 4 patties. Lower the heat on the air fryer to 180ºC. Arrange the burgers in a single layer in the basket of the air fryer. Pausing halfway through the cooking time to turn the burgers, air fry for 10 minutes, or until a thermometer inserted into the thickest part registers 70ºC. Top the burgers with the cheese slices and continue baking for a minute or two, just until the cheese has melted. Serve the burgers on a lettuce leaf topped with the roasted peppers.

## Bo Luc Lac

**Prep time: 50 minutes | Cook time: 8 minutes | Serves 4**

For the Meat:
2 teaspoons soy sauce
4 garlic cloves, minced
1 teaspoon coarse or flaky salt
2 teaspoons sugar
¼ teaspoon ground black
pepper
1 teaspoon toasted sesame oil
680 g top rump steak, cut into
1-inch cubes
Cooking spray
For the Salad:
1 head butterhead lettuce,
leaves separated and torn into
large pieces
60 ml fresh mint leaves

120 ml halved baby plum
tomatoes
½ red onion, halved and thinly
sliced
2 tablespoons apple cider
vinegar
1 garlic clove, minced
2 teaspoons sugar
¼ teaspoon coarse or flaky salt
¼ teaspoon ground black
pepper
2 tablespoons vegetable oil
For Serving:
Lime wedges, for garnish
Coarse salt and freshly cracked
black pepper, to taste

Combine the ingredients for the meat, except for the steak, in a large bowl. Stir to mix well. Dunk the steak cubes in the bowl and press to coat. Wrap the bowl in plastic and marinate under room temperature for at least 30 minutes. Preheat the air fryer to 230ºC. Spritz the air fryer basket with cooking spray. Discard the marinade and transfer the steak cubes in the preheated air fryer basket. You need to air fry in batches to avoid overcrowding. Air fry for 4 minutes or until the steak cubes are lightly browned but still have a little pink. Shake the basket halfway through the cooking time. Meanwhile, combine the ingredients for the salad in a separate large bowl. Toss to mix well. Pour the salad in a large serving bowl and top with the steak cubes. Squeeze the lime wedges over and sprinkle with salt and black pepper before serving.

## Kheema Burgers

**Prep time: 15 minutes | Cook time: 12 minutes | Serves 4**

Burgers:
450 g 85% lean beef mince or lamb mince
2 large eggs, lightly beaten
1 medium brown onion, diced
60 ml chopped fresh coriander
1 tablespoon minced fresh ginger
3 cloves garlic, minced
2 teaspoons garam masala
1 teaspoon ground turmeric
½ teaspoon ground cinnamon

⅛ teaspoon ground cardamom
1 teaspoon coarse or flaky salt
1 teaspoon cayenne pepper
Raita Sauce:
235 ml grated cucumber
120 ml sour cream
¼ teaspoon coarse or flaky salt
¼ teaspoon black pepper
For Serving:
4 lettuce leaves, hamburger buns, or naan breads

For the burgers: In a large bowl, combine the beef mince, eggs, onion, coriander, ginger, garlic, garam masala, turmeric, cinnamon, cardamom, salt, and cayenne. Gently mix until ingredients are thoroughly combined. Divide the meat into four portions and form into round patties. Make a slight depression in the middle of each patty with your thumb to prevent them from puffing up into a dome shape while cooking. Place the patties in the air fryer basket. Set the air fryer to 175ºC for 12 minutes. Use a meat thermometer to ensure the burgers have reached an internal temperature of 70ºC (for medium). Meanwhile, for the sauce: In a small bowl, combine the cucumber, sour cream, salt, and pepper. To serve: Place the burgers on the lettuce, buns, or naan and top with the sauce.

## Nigerian Peanut-Crusted Bavette Steak

**Prep time: 30 minutes | Cook time: 8 minutes | Serves 4**

Suya Spice Mix:
60 ml dry-roasted peanuts
1 teaspoon cumin seeds
1 teaspoon garlic powder
1 teaspoon smoked paprika
½ teaspoon ground ginger

1 teaspoon coarse or flaky salt
½ teaspoon cayenne pepper
Steak:
450 g bavette or skirt steak
2 tablespoons vegetable oil

For the spice mix: In a clean coffee grinder or spice mill, combine the peanuts and cumin seeds. Process until you get a coarse powder. (Do not overprocess or you will wind up with peanut butter! Alternatively, you can grind the cumin with 80 ml ready-made peanut powder instead of the peanuts.) Pour the peanut mixture into a small bowl, add the garlic powder, paprika, ginger, salt, and cayenne, and stir to combine. This recipe makes about 120 ml suya spice mix. Store leftovers in an airtight container in a cool, dry place for up to 1 month. For the steak: Cut the steak into ½-inch-thick slices, cutting against the grain and at a slight angle. Place the beef strips in a resealable plastic bag and add the oil and 2½ to 3 tablespoons of the spice mixture. Seal the bag and massage to coat all of the meat with the oil and spice mixture. Marinate at room temperature for 30 minutes or in the refrigerator for up to 24 hours. Place the beef strips in the air fryer basket. Set the air fryer to 200ºC for 8 minutes, turning the strips halfway through the cooking time. Transfer the meat to a serving platter. Sprinkle with additional spice mix, if desired.

## Italian Sausage and Cheese Meatballs

**Prep time: 10 minutes | Cook time: 20 minutes | Serves 4**

230 g sausage meat with Italian seasoning added to taste
230 g 85% lean beef mince
120 ml shredded sharp Cheddar

cheese
½ teaspoon onion granules
½ teaspoon garlic powder
½ teaspoon black pepper

In a large bowl, gently mix the sausage meat, beef mince, cheese, onion granules, garlic powder, and pepper until well combined. Form the mixture into 16 meatballs. Place the meatballs in a single layer in the air fryer basket. Set the air fryer to 175ºC for 20 minutes, turning the meatballs halfway through the cooking time. Use a meat thermometer to ensure the meatballs have reached an internal temperature of 70ºC (medium).

## Spice-Rubbed Pork Loin

**Prep time: 5 minutes | Cook time: 20 minutes | Serves 6**

1 teaspoon paprika
½ teaspoon ground cumin
½ teaspoon chili powder
½ teaspoon garlic powder
2 tablespoons coconut oil

1 (680 g) boneless pork loin
½ teaspoon salt
¼ teaspoon ground black pepper

In a small bowl, mix paprika, cumin, chili powder, and garlic powder. Drizzle coconut oil over pork. Sprinkle pork loin with salt and pepper, then rub spice mixture evenly on all sides. Place pork loin into ungreased air fryer basket. Adjust the temperature to 200ºC and air fry for 20 minutes, turning pork halfway through cooking. Pork loin will be browned and have an internal temperature of at least 65ºC when done. Serve warm.

## Honey-Baked Pork Loin

**Prep time: 30 minutes | Cook time: 22 to 25 minutes | Serves 6**

60 ml honey
60 ml freshly squeezed lemon juice
2 tablespoons soy sauce

1 teaspoon garlic powder
1 (900 g) pork loin
2 tablespoons vegetable oil

In a medium bowl, whisk together the honey, lemon juice, soy sauce, and garlic powder. Reserve half of the mixture for basting during cooking. Cut 5 slits in the pork loin and transfer it to a resealable bag. Add the remaining honey mixture. Seal the bag and refrigerate to marinate for at least 2 hours. Preheat the air fryer to 200ºC. Line the air fryer basket with parchment paper. Remove the pork from the marinade, and place it on the parchment. Spritz with oil, then baste with the reserved marinade. Cook for 15 minutes. Flip the pork, baste with more marinade and spritz with oil again. Cook for 7 to 10 minutes more until the internal temperature reaches 65ºC. Let rest for 5 minutes before serving.

## Smothered Chops

**Prep time: 20 minutes | Cook time: 30 minutes | Serves 4**

4 bone-in pork chops (230 g each)
2 teaspoons salt, divided
1½ teaspoons freshly ground black pepper, divided
1 teaspoon garlic powder
235 ml tomato purée

1½ teaspoons Italian seasoning
1 tablespoon sugar
1 tablespoon cornflour
120 ml chopped onion
120 ml chopped green pepper
1 to 2 tablespoons oil

Evenly season the pork chops with 1 teaspoon salt, 1 teaspoon pepper, and the garlic powder. In a medium bowl, stir together the tomato purée, Italian seasoning, sugar, remaining 1 teaspoon of salt, and remaining ½ teaspoon of pepper. In a small bowl, whisk 180 ml water and the cornflour until blended. Stir this slurry into the tomato purée, with the onion and green pepper. Transfer to a baking pan. Preheat the air fryer to 175°C. Place the sauce in the fryer and cook for 10 minutes. Stir and cook for 10 minutes more. Remove the pan and keep warm. Increase the air fryer temperature to 200°C. Line the air fryer basket with parchment paper. Place the pork chops on the parchment and spritz with oil. Cook for 5 minutes. Flip and spritz the chops with oil and cook for 5 minutes more, until the internal temperature reaches 65°C. Serve with the tomato mixture spooned on top.

## Bacon and Cheese Stuffed Pork Chops

**Prep time: 10 minutes | Cook time: 12 minutes | Serves 4**

15 g plain pork scratchings, finely crushed
120 ml shredded sharp Cheddar cheese
4 slices cooked bacon,

crumbled
4 (110 g) boneless pork chops
½ teaspoon salt
¼ teaspoon ground black pepper

In a small bowl, mix pork scratchings, Cheddar, and bacon. Make a 3-inch slit in the side of each pork chop and stuff with ¼ pork rind mixture. Sprinkle each side of pork chops with salt and pepper. Place pork chops into ungreased air fryer basket, stuffed side up. Adjust the temperature to 200°C and air fry for 12 minutes. Pork chops will be browned and have an internal temperature of at least 65°C when done. Serve warm.

## Spicy Bavette Steak with Zhoug

**Prep time: 30 minutes | Cook time: 8 minutes | Serves 4**

Marinade and Steak:
120 ml dark beer or orange juice
60 ml fresh lemon juice
3 cloves garlic, minced
2 tablespoons extra-virgin olive oil
2 tablespoons Sriracha
2 tablespoons brown sugar
2 teaspoons ground cumin

2 teaspoons smoked paprika
1 tablespoon coarse or flaky salt
1 teaspoon black pepper
680 g bavette or skirt steak, trimmed and cut into 3 pieces
Zhoug:
235 ml packed fresh coriander leaves
2 cloves garlic, peeled
2 jalapeño or green chiles,

stemmed and coarsely chopped
½ teaspoon ground cumin
¼ teaspoon ground coriander

¼ teaspoon coarse or flaky salt
2 to 4 tablespoons extra-virgin olive oil

For the marinade and steak: In a small bowl, whisk together the beer, lemon juice, garlic, olive oil, Sriracha, brown sugar, cumin, paprika, salt, and pepper. Place the steak in a large resealable plastic bag. Pour the marinade over the steak, seal the bag, and massage the steak to coat. Marinate in the refrigerator for 1 hour or up to 24 hours, turning the bag occasionally. Meanwhile, for the zhoug: In a food processor, combine the coriander, garlic, jalapeños, cumin, coriander, and salt. Process until finely chopped. Add 2 tablespoons olive oil and pulse to form a loose paste, adding up to 2 tablespoons more olive oil if needed. Transfer the zhoug to a glass container. Cover and store in the refrigerator until 30 minutes before serving if marinating more than 1 hour. Remove the steak from the marinade and discard the marinade. Place the steak in the air fryer basket and set the air fryer to 200°C for 8 minutes. Use a meat thermometer to ensure the steak has reached an internal temperature of 65°C (for medium). Transfer the steak to a cutting board and let rest for 5 minutes. Slice the steak across the grain and serve with the zhoug.

## Kielbasa Sausage with Pineapple and Peppers

**Prep time: 15 minutes | Cook time: 10 minutes | Serves 2 to 4**

340 g kielbasa sausage, cut into ½-inch slices
1 (230 g) can pineapple chunks in juice, drained
235 ml pepper chunks

1 tablespoon barbecue seasoning
1 tablespoon soy sauce
Cooking spray

Preheat the air fryer to 200°C. Spritz the air fryer basket with cooking spray. Combine all the ingredients in a large bowl. Toss to mix well. Pour the sausage mixture in the preheated air fryer. Air fry for 10 minutes or until the sausage is lightly browned and the pepper and pineapple are soft. Shake the basket halfway through. Serve immediately.

## Bacon-Wrapped Vegetable Kebabs

**Prep time: 10 minutes | Cook time: 10 to 12 minutes | Serves 4**

110 g mushrooms, sliced
1 small courgette, sliced
12 baby plum tomatoes
110 g sliced bacon, halved

Avocado oil spray
Sea salt and freshly ground black pepper, to taste

Stack 3 mushroom slices, 1 courgette slice, and 1 tomato. Wrap a bacon strip around the vegetables and thread them onto a skewer. Repeat with the remaining vegetables and bacon. Spray with oil and sprinkle with salt and pepper. Set the air fryer to 200°C. Place the skewers in the air fryer basket in a single layer, working in batches if necessary, and air fry for 5 minutes. Flip the skewers and cook for 5 to 7 minutes more, until the bacon is crispy and the vegetables are tender. Serve warm.

## Garlic Butter Steak Bites

**Prep time: 5 minutes | Cook time: 16 minutes | Serves 3**

| | |
|---|---|
| Oil, for spraying | sauce |
| 450 g boneless steak, cut into | ½ teaspoon granulated garlic |
| 1-inch pieces | ½ teaspoon salt |
| 2 tablespoons olive oil | ¼ teaspoon freshly ground |
| 1 teaspoon Worcestershire | black pepper |

Preheat the air fryer to 200ºC. Line the air fryer basket with parchment and spray lightly with oil. In a medium bowl, combine the steak, olive oil, Worcestershire sauce, garlic, salt, and black pepper and toss until evenly coated. Place the steak in a single layer in the prepared basket. You may have to work in batches, depending on the size of your air fryer. Cook for 10 to 16 minutes, flipping every 3 to 4 minutes. The total cooking time will depend on the thickness of the meat and your preferred doneness. If you want it well done, it may take up to 5 additional minutes.

## Kielbasa and Cabbage

**Prep time: 10 minutes | Cook time: 20 to 25 minutes | Serves 4**

| | |
|---|---|
| 450 g smoked kielbasa sausage, sliced into ½-inch pieces | 2 tablespoons olive oil |
| 1 head cabbage, very coarsely chopped | ½ teaspoon salt |
| ½ brown onion, chopped | ½ teaspoon freshly ground black pepper |
| 2 cloves garlic, chopped | 60 ml water |

Preheat the air fryer to 200ºC. In a large bowl, combine the sausage, cabbage, onion, garlic, olive oil, salt, and black pepper. Toss until thoroughly combined. Transfer the mixture to the basket of the air fryer and pour the water over the top. Pausing two or three times during the cooking time to shake the basket, air fry for 20 to 25 minutes, until the sausage is browned and the vegetables are tender.

## Steaks with Walnut-Blue Cheese Butter

**Prep time: 30 minutes | Cook time: 10 minutes | Serves 6**

| | |
|---|---|
| 120 ml unsalted butter, at room temperature | 1 teaspoon minced garlic |
| 120 ml crumbled blue cheese | ¼ teaspoon cayenne pepper |
| 2 tablespoons finely chopped walnuts | Sea salt and freshly ground black pepper, to taste |
| 1 tablespoon minced fresh rosemary | 680 g sirloin steaks, at room temperature |

In a medium bowl, combine the butter, blue cheese, walnuts, rosemary, garlic, and cayenne pepper and salt and black pepper to taste. Use clean hands to ensure that everything is well combined. Place the mixture on a sheet of parchment paper and form it into a log. Wrap it tightly in plastic wrap. Refrigerate for at least 2 hours or freeze for 30 minutes. Season the steaks generously with salt and pepper. Place the air fryer basket or grill pan in the air fryer. Set the air fryer to 200ºC and let it preheat for 5 minutes. Place the steaks in the basket in a single layer and air fry for 5 minutes. Flip the steaks, and cook for 5 minutes more, until an instant-read thermometer reads 50ºC for medium-rare (or as desired). Transfer the steaks to a plate. Cut the butter into pieces and place the desired amount on top of the steaks. Tent a piece of aluminum foil over the steaks and allow to sit for 10 minutes before serving. Store any remaining butter in a sealed container in the refrigerator for up to 2 weeks.

## Ketchup Sauce

**Prep time: 5 minutes | Cook time: 10 to 12 minutes | Serves 5**

| | |
|---|---|
| 10 thin slices of bacon | 60 ml mayonnaise |
| 5 pork hot dogs, halved | 4 tablespoons ketchup |
| 1 teaspoon cayenne pepper | 1 teaspoon rice vinegar |
| Sauce: | 1 teaspoon chili powder |

Preheat the air fryer to 200ºC. Arrange the slices of bacon on a clean work surface. One by one, place the halved hot dog on one end of each slice, season with cayenne pepper and wrap the hot dog with the bacon slices and secure with toothpicks as needed. Work in batches, place half the wrapped hot dogs in the air fryer basket and air fry for 10 to 12 minutes or until the bacon becomes browned and crispy. Make the sauce: Stir all the ingredients for the sauce in a small bowl. Wrap the bowl in plastic and set in the refrigerator until ready to serve. Transfer the hot dogs to a platter and serve hot with the sauce.

## Lebanese Malfouf (Stuffed Cabbage Rolls)

**Prep time: 15 minutes | Cook time: 33 minutes | Serves 4**

| | |
|---|---|
| 1 head green cabbage | 2 tablespoons chopped fresh mint |
| 450 g lean beef mince | Juice of 1 lemon |
| 120 ml long-grain brown rice | Olive oil cooking spray |
| 4 garlic cloves, minced | 120 ml beef stock |
| 1 teaspoon salt | 1 tablespoon olive oil |
| ½ teaspoon black pepper | |
| 1 teaspoon ground cinnamon | |

Cut the cabbage in half and remove the core. Remove 12 of the larger leaves to use for the cabbage rolls. Bring a large pot of salted water to a boil, then drop the cabbage leaves into the water, boiling them for 3 minutes. Remove from the water and set aside. In a large bowl, combine the beef, rice, garlic, salt, pepper, cinnamon, mint, and lemon juice, and mix together until combined. Divide this mixture into 12 equal portions. Preheat the air fryer to 180ºC. Lightly coat a small casserole dish with olive oil cooking spray. Place a cabbage leaf on a clean work surface. Place a spoonful of the beef mixture on one side of the leaf, leaving space on all other sides. Fold the two perpendicular sides inward and then roll forward, tucking tightly as rolled (similar to a burrito roll). Place the finished rolls into the baking dish, stacking them on top of each other if needed. Pour the beef stock over the top of the cabbage rolls so that it soaks down between them, and then brush the tops with the olive oil. Place the casserole dish into the air fryer basket and bake for 30 minutes.

## Minute Steak Roll-Ups

| | |
|---|---|
| 4 minute steaks (170 g each) | onion |
| 1 (450 g) bottle Italian dressing | 120 ml finely chopped green |
| 1 teaspoon salt | pepper |
| ½ teaspoon freshly ground | 120 ml finely chopped |
| black pepper | mushrooms |
| 120 ml finely chopped brown | 1 to 2 tablespoons oil |

In a large resealable bag or airtight storage container, combine the steaks and Italian dressing. Seal the bag and refrigerate to marinate for 2 hours. Remove the steaks from the marinade and place them on a cutting board. Discard the marinade. Evenly season the steaks with salt and pepper. In a small bowl, stir together the onion, pepper, and mushrooms. Sprinkle the onion mixture evenly over the steaks. Roll up the steaks, jelly roll-style, and secure with toothpicks. Preheat the air fryer to 200ºC. Place the steaks in the air fryer basket. Cook for 4 minutes. Flip the steaks and spritz them with oil. Cook for 4 to 6 minutes more until the internal temperature reaches 65ºC. Let rest for 5 minutes before serving.

## Sausage and Cauliflower Arancini

| | |
|---|---|
| Avocado oil spray | 85 g cream cheese |
| 170 g Italian-seasoned sausage, | 110 g Cheddar cheese, shredded |
| casings removed | 1 large egg |
| 60 ml diced onion | 120 ml finely ground blanched |
| 1 teaspoon minced garlic | almond flour |
| 1 teaspoon dried thyme | 60 ml finely grated Parmesan |
| Sea salt and freshly ground | cheese |
| black pepper, to taste | Keto-friendly marinara sauce, |
| 120 ml cauliflower rice | for serving |

Spray a large skillet with oil and place it over medium-high heat. Once the skillet is hot, put the sausage in the skillet and cook for 7 minutes, breaking up the meat with the back of a spoon. Reduce the heat to medium and add the onion. Cook for 5 minutes, then add the garlic, thyme, and salt and pepper to taste. Cook for 1 minute more. Add the cauliflower rice and cream cheese to the skillet. Cook for 7 minutes, stirring frequently, until the cream cheese melts and the cauliflower is tender. Remove the skillet from the heat and stir in the Cheddar cheese. Using a cookie scoop, form the mixture into 1½-inch balls. Place the balls on a parchment paper-lined baking sheet. Freeze for 30 minutes. Place the egg in a shallow bowl and beat it with a fork. In a separate bowl, stir together the almond flour and Parmesan cheese. Dip the cauliflower balls into the egg, then coat them with the almond flour mixture, gently pressing the mixture to the balls to adhere. Set the air fryer to 200ºC. Spray the cauliflower rice balls with oil, and arrange them in a single layer in the air fryer basket, working in batches if necessary. Air fry for 5 minutes. Flip the rice balls and spray them with more oil. Air fry for 3 to 7 minutes longer, until the balls are golden brown. Serve warm with marinara sauce.

## Mojito Lamb Chops

| | |
|---|---|
| Marinade: | 2 teaspoons fine sea salt |
| 2 teaspoons grated lime zest | ½ teaspoon ground black |
| 120 ml lime juice | pepper |
| 60 ml avocado oil | 4 (1-inch-thick) lamb chops |
| 60 ml chopped fresh mint | Sprigs of fresh mint, for garnish |
| leaves | (optional) |
| 4 cloves garlic, roughly | Lime slices, for serving |
| chopped | (optional) |

Make the marinade: Place all the ingredients for the marinade in a food processor or blender and purée until mostly smooth with a few small chunks. Transfer half of the marinade to a shallow dish and set the other half aside for serving. Add the lamb to the shallow dish, cover, and place in the refrigerator to marinate for at least 2 hours or overnight. Spray the air fryer basket with avocado oil. Preheat the air fryer to 200ºC. Remove the chops from the marinade and place them in the air fryer basket. Air fry for 5 minutes, or until the internal temperature reaches 65ºC for medium doneness. Allow the chops to rest for 10 minutes before serving with the rest of the marinade as a sauce. Garnish with fresh mint leaves and serve with lime slices, if desired. Best served fresh.

## Five-Spice Pork Belly

| | |
|---|---|
| 450 g unsalted pork belly | 2 cloves garlic, minced |
| 2 teaspoons Chinese five-spice | 120 ml beef or chicken stock |
| powder | ¼ to 120 ml liquid or powdered |
| Sauce: | sweetener |
| 1 tablespoon coconut oil | 3 tablespoons wheat-free tamari |
| 1 (1-inch) piece fresh ginger, | 1 spring onion, sliced, plus |
| peeled and grated | more for garnish |

Spray the air fryer basket with avocado oil. Preheat the air fryer to 200ºC. Cut the pork belly into ½-inch-thick slices and season well on all sides with the five-spice powder. Place the slices in a single layer in the air fryer basket (if you're using a smaller air fryer, work in batches if necessary) and cook for 8 minutes, or until cooked to your liking, flipping halfway through. While the pork belly cooks, make the sauce: Heat the coconut oil in a small saucepan over medium heat. Add the ginger and garlic and sauté for 1 minute, or until fragrant. Add the stock, sweetener, and tamari and simmer for 10 to 15 minutes, until thickened. Add the spring onion and cook for another minute, until the spring onion is softened. Taste and adjust the seasoning to your liking. Transfer the pork belly to a large bowl. Pour the sauce over the pork belly and coat well. Place the pork belly slices on a serving platter and garnish with sliced spring onions. Best served fresh. Store leftovers in an airtight container in the fridge for up to 4 days. Reheat in a preheated 200ºC air fryer for 3 minutes, or until heated through.

## Sweet and Spicy Country-Style Ribs

**Prep time: 10 minutes | Cook time: 25 minutes | Serves 4**

| | |
|---|---|
| 2 tablespoons brown sugar | 1 teaspoon coarse or flaky salt |
| 2 tablespoons smoked paprika | 1 teaspoon black pepper |
| 1 teaspoon garlic powder | ¼ to ½ teaspoon cayenne |
| 1 teaspoon onion granules | pepper |
| 1 teaspoon mustard powder | 680 g boneless pork steaks |
| 1 teaspoon ground cumin | 235 ml barbecue sauce |

In a small bowl, stir together the brown sugar, paprika, garlic powder, onion granules, mustard powder, cumin, salt, black pepper, and cayenne. Mix until well combined. Pat the ribs dry with a paper towel. Generously sprinkle the rub evenly over both sides of the ribs and rub in with your fingers. Place the ribs in the air fryer basket. Set the air fryer to 175°C for 15 minutes. Turn the ribs and brush with 120 ml of the barbecue sauce. Cook for an additional 10 minutes. Use a meat thermometer to ensure the pork has reached an internal temperature of 65°C. Serve with remaining barbecue sauce.

## Kheema Meatloaf

**Prep time: 10 minutes | Cook time: 15 minutes | Serves 4**

| | |
|---|---|
| 450 g 85% lean beef mince | 2 teaspoons garam masala |
| 2 large eggs, lightly beaten | 1 teaspoon coarse or flaky salt |
| 235 ml diced brown onion | 1 teaspoon ground turmeric |
| 60 ml chopped fresh coriander | 1 teaspoon cayenne pepper |
| 1 tablespoon minced fresh | ½ teaspoon ground cinnamon |
| ginger | ⅛ teaspoon ground cardamom |
| 1 tablespoon minced garlic | |

In a large bowl, gently mix the beef mince, eggs, onion, coriander, ginger, garlic, garam masala, salt, turmeric, cayenne, cinnamon, and cardamom until thoroughly combined. Place the seasoned meat in a baking pan. Place the pan in the air fryer basket. Set the air fryer to 175°C for 15 minutes. Use a meat thermometer to ensure the meat loaf has reached an internal temperature of 70°C (medium). Drain the fat and liquid from the pan and let stand for 5 minutes before slicing. Slice and serve hot.

## Pepper Steak

**Prep time: 30 minutes | Cook time: 16 to 20 minutes | Serves 4**

| | |
|---|---|
| 450 g minute steak, cut into | black pepper |
| 1-inch pieces | 60 ml cornflour |
| 235 ml Italian dressing | 235 ml thinly sliced pepper, any |
| 355 ml beef stock | color |
| 1 tablespoon soy sauce | 235 ml chopped celery |
| ½ teaspoon salt | 1 tablespoon minced garlic |
| ¼ teaspoon freshly ground | 1 to 2 tablespoons oil |

In a large resealable bag, combine the beef and Italian dressing. Seal the bag and refrigerate to marinate for 8 hours. In a small bowl, whisk the beef stock, soy sauce, salt, and pepper until blended. In another small bowl, whisk 60 ml water and the cornflour until dissolved. Stir the cornflour mixture into the beef stock mixture until blended. Preheat the air fryer to 190°C. Pour the stock mixture into a baking pan. Cook for 4 minutes. Stir and cook for 4 to 5 minutes more. Remove and set aside. Increase the air fryer temperature to 200°C. Line the air fryer basket with parchment paper. Remove the steak from the marinade and place it in a medium bowl. Discard the marinade. Stir in the pepper, celery, and garlic. Place the steak and pepper mixture on the parchment. Spritz with oil. Cook for 4 minutes. Shake the basket and cook for 4 to 7 minutes more, until the vegetables are tender and the meat reaches an internal temperature of 65°C. Serve with the gravy.

## Mongolian-Style Beef

**Prep time: 10 minutes | Cook time: 10 minutes | Serves 4**

| | |
|---|---|
| Oil, for spraying | 2 teaspoons toasted sesame oil |
| 60 ml cornflour | 1 tablespoon minced garlic |
| 450 g bavette or skirt steak, | ½ teaspoon ground ginger |
| thinly sliced | 120 ml water |
| 180 ml packed light brown | Cooked white rice or ramen |
| sugar | noodles, for serving |
| 120 ml soy sauce | |

Line the air fryer basket with parchment and spray lightly with oil. Place the cornflour in a bowl and dredge the steak until evenly coated. Shake off any excess cornflour. Place the steak in the prepared basket and spray lightly with oil. Roast at 200°C for 5 minutes, flip, and cook for another 5 minutes. In a small saucepan, combine the brown sugar, soy sauce, sesame oil, garlic, ginger, and water and bring to a boil over medium-high heat, stirring frequently. Remove from the heat. Transfer the meat to the sauce and toss until evenly coated. Let sit for about 5 minutes so the steak absorbs the flavors. Serve with white rice or ramen noodles.

## Panko Crusted Calf's Liver Strips

**Prep time: 15 minutes | Cook time: 23 to 25 minutes | Serves 4**

| | |
|---|---|
| 450 g sliced calf's liver, cut into | 475 ml panko breadcrumbs |
| ½-inch wide strips | Salt and ground black pepper, |
| 2 eggs | to taste |
| 2 tablespoons milk | Cooking spray |
| 120 ml whole wheat flour | |

Preheat the air fryer to 200°C and spritz with cooking spray. Rub the calf's liver strips with salt and ground black pepper on a clean work surface. Whisk the eggs with milk in a large bowl. Pour the flour in a shallow dish. Pour the panko on a separate shallow dish. Dunk the liver strips in the flour, then in the egg mixture. Shake the excess off and roll the strips over the panko to coat well. Arrange half of the liver strips in a single layer in the preheated air fryer and spritz with cooking spray. Air fry for 5 minutes or until browned. Flip the strips halfway through. Repeat with the remaining strips. Serve immediately.

## Bacon-Wrapped Hot Dogs with Mayo-Ritzy Skirt Steak Fajitas

**Prep time: 15 minutes | Cook time: 30 minutes | Serves 4**

2 tablespoons olive oil
60 ml lime juice
1 clove garlic, minced
½ teaspoon ground cumin
½ teaspoon hot sauce
½ teaspoon salt
2 tablespoons chopped fresh coriander
450 g skirt steak
1 onion, sliced
1 teaspoon chili powder
1 red pepper, sliced

1 green pepper, sliced
Salt and freshly ground black pepper, to taste
8 flour tortillas
Toppings:
Shredded lettuce
Crumbled feta or ricotta (or grated Cheddar cheese)
Sliced black olives
Diced tomatoes
Sour cream
Guacamole

Combine the olive oil, lime juice, garlic, cumin, hot sauce, salt and coriander in a shallow dish. Add the skirt steak and turn it over several times to coat all sides. Pierce the steak with a needle-style meat tenderizer or paring knife. Marinate the steak in the refrigerator for at least 3 hours, or overnight. When you are ready to cook, remove the steak from the refrigerator and let it sit at room temperature for 30 minutes. Preheat the air fryer to 200ºC. Toss the onion slices with the chili powder and a little olive oil and transfer them to the air fryer basket. Air fry for 5 minutes. Add the red and green peppers to the air fryer basket with the onions, season with salt and pepper and air fry for 8 more minutes, until the onions and peppers are soft. Transfer the vegetables to a dish and cover with aluminum foil to keep warm. Put the skirt steak in the air fryer basket and pour the marinade over the top. Air fry at 200ºC for 12 minutes. Flip the steak over and air fry for an additional 5 minutes. Transfer the cooked steak to a cutting board and let the steak rest for a few minutes. If the peppers and onions need to be heated, return them to the air fryer for just 1 to 2 minutes. Thinly slice the steak at an angle, cutting against the grain of the steak. Serve the steak with the onions and peppers, the warm tortillas and the fajita toppings on the side.

## Rosemary Ribeye Steaks

**Prep time: 10 minutes | Cook time: 15 minutes | Serves 2**

60 ml butter
1 clove garlic, minced
Salt and ground black pepper, to taste

1½ tablespoons balsamic vinegar
60 ml rosemary, chopped
2 ribeye steaks

Melt the butter in a skillet over medium heat. Add the garlic and fry until fragrant. Remove the skillet from the heat and add the salt, pepper, and vinegar. Allow it to cool. Add the rosemary, then pour the mixture into a Ziploc bag. Put the ribeye steaks in the bag and shake well, coating the meat well. Refrigerate for an hour, then allow to sit for a further twenty minutes. Preheat the air fryer to 200ºC. Air fry the ribeye steaks for 15 minutes. Take care when removing the steaks from the air fryer and plate up. Serve immediately.

## Blue Cheese Steak Salad

**Prep time: 30 minutes | Cook time: 22 minutes | Serves 4**

2 tablespoons balsamic vinegar
2 tablespoons red wine vinegar
1 tablespoon Dijon mustard
1 tablespoon granulated sweetener
1 teaspoon minced garlic
Sea salt and freshly ground black pepper, to taste

180 ml extra-virgin olive oil
450 g boneless rump steak
Avocado oil spray
1 small red onion, cut into ¼-inch-thick rounds
170 g baby spinach
120 ml cherry tomatoes, halved
85 g blue cheese, crumbled

In a blender, combine the balsamic vinegar, red wine vinegar, Dijon mustard, sweetener, and garlic. Season with salt and pepper and process until smooth. With the blender running, drizzle in the olive oil. Process until well combined. Transfer to a jar with a tight-fitting lid, and refrigerate until ready to serve (it will keep for up to 2 weeks). Season the steak with salt and pepper and let sit at room temperature for at least 45 minutes, time permitting. Set the air fryer to 200ºC. Spray the steak with oil and place it in the air fryer basket. Air fry for 6 minutes. Flip the steak and spray it with more oil. Air fry for 6 minutes more for medium-rare or until the steak is done to your liking. Transfer the steak to a plate, tent with a piece of aluminum foil, and allow it to rest. Spray the onion slices with oil and place them in the air fryer basket. Cook at 200ºC for 5 minutes. Flip the onion slices and spray them with more oil. Air fry for 5 minutes more. Slice the steak diagonally into thin strips. Place the spinach, cherry tomatoes, onion slices, and steak in a large bowl. Toss with the desired amount of dressing. Sprinkle with crumbled blue cheese and serve.

## Italian Sausages with Peppers and Onions

**Prep time: 5 minutes | Cook time: 28 minutes | Serves 3**

1 medium onion, thinly sliced
1 yellow or orange pepper, thinly sliced
1 red pepper, thinly sliced
60 ml avocado oil or melted

coconut oil
1 teaspoon fine sea salt
6 Italian-seasoned sausages
Dijon mustard, for serving (optional)

Preheat the air fryer to 200ºC. Place the onion and peppers in a large bowl. Drizzle with the oil and toss well to coat the veggies. Season with the salt. Place the onion and peppers in a pie pan and cook in the air fryer for 8 minutes, stirring halfway through. Remove from the air fryer and set aside. Spray the air fryer basket with avocado oil. Place the sausages in the air fryer basket and air fry for 20 minutes, or until crispy and golden brown. During the last minute or two of cooking, add the onion and peppers to the basket with the sausages to warm them through. Place the onion and peppers on a serving platter and arrange the sausages on top. Serve Dijon mustard on the side, if desired. Store leftovers in an airtight container in the fridge for up to 7 days or in the freezer for up to a month. Reheat in a preheated 200ºC air fryer for 3 minutes, or until heated through.

## Spicy Rump Steak

**Prep time: 25 minutes | Cook time: 12 to 18 minutes | Serves 4**

2 tablespoons salsa
1 tablespoon minced chipotle pepper or chipotle paste
1 tablespoon apple cider vinegar
1 teaspoon ground cumin
⅛ teaspoon freshly ground black pepper
⅛ teaspoon red pepper flakes
340 g rump steak, cut into 4 pieces and gently pounded to about ⅓ inch thick
Cooking oil spray

In a small bowl, thoroughly mix the salsa, chipotle pepper, vinegar, cumin, black pepper, and red pepper flakes. Rub this mixture into both sides of each steak piece. Let stand for 15 minutes at room temperature. Insert the crisper plate into the basket and place the basket into the unit. Preheat the unit by selecting AIR FRY, setting the temperature to 200ºC, and setting the time to 3 minutes. Select START/STOP to begin. Once the unit is preheated, spray the crisper plate with cooking oil. Working in batches, place 2 steaks into the basket. Select AIR FRY, set the temperature to 200ºC, and set the time to 9 minutes. Select START/STOP to begin. After about 6 minutes, check the steaks. If a food thermometer inserted into the meat registers at least 65ºC, they are done. If not, resume cooking. When the cooking is done, transfer the steaks to a clean plate and cover with aluminum foil to keep warm. Repeat steps 3, 4, and 5 with the remaining steaks. Thinly slice the steaks against the grain and serve.

## Cheesy Low-Carb Lasagna

**Prep time: 10 minutes | Cook time: 10 minutes | Serves 4**

Meat Layer:
Extra-virgin olive oil
450 g 85% lean beef mince
235 ml marinara sauce
60 ml diced celery
60 ml diced red onion
½ teaspoon minced garlic
Coarse or flaky salt and black pepper, to taste
Cheese Layer:
230 g ricotta cheese
235 ml shredded Mozzarella cheese
120 ml grated Parmesan cheese
2 large eggs
1 teaspoon dried Italian seasoning, crushed
½ teaspoon each minced garlic, garlic powder, and black pepper

For the meat layer: Grease a cake pan with 1 teaspoon olive oil. In a large bowl, combine the beef mince, marinara, celery, onion, garlic, salt, and pepper. Place the seasoned meat in the pan. Place the pan in the air fryer basket. Set the air fryer to 190ºC for 10 minutes. Meanwhile, for the cheese layer: In a medium bowl, combine the ricotta, half the Mozzarella, the Parmesan, lightly beaten eggs, Italian seasoning, minced garlic, garlic powder, and pepper. Stir until well blended. At the end of the cooking time, spread the cheese mixture over the meat mixture. Sprinkle with the remaining 120 ml Mozzarella. Set the air fryer to 190ºC for 10 minutes, or until the cheese is browned and bubbling. At the end of the cooking time, use a meat thermometer to ensure the meat has reached an internal temperature of 70ºC. Drain the fat and liquid from the pan. Let stand for 5 minutes before serving.

## Herb-Crusted Lamb Chops

**Prep time: 10 minutes | Cook time: 5 minutes | Serves 2**

1 large egg
2 cloves garlic, minced
60 ml finely crushed pork scratchings
60 ml pre-grated Parmesan cheese
1 tablespoon chopped fresh oregano leaves
1 tablespoon chopped fresh rosemary leaves
1 teaspoon chopped fresh thyme leaves
½ teaspoon ground black pepper
4 (1-inch-thick) lamb chops
For Garnish/Serving (Optional):
Sprigs of fresh oregano
Sprigs of fresh rosemary
Sprigs of fresh thyme
Lavender flowers
Lemon slices

Spray the air fryer basket with avocado oil. Preheat the air fryer to 200ºC. Beat the egg in a shallow bowl, add the garlic, and stir well to combine. In another shallow bowl, mix together the crushed pork scratchings, Parmesan, herbs, and pepper. One at a time, dip the lamb chops into the egg mixture, shake off the excess egg, and then dredge them in the Parmesan mixture. Use your hands to coat the chops well in the Parmesan mixture and form a nice crust on all sides; if necessary, dip the chops again in both the egg and the Parmesan mixture. Place the lamb chops in the air fryer basket, leaving space between them, and air fry for 5 minutes, or until the internal temperature reaches 65ºC for medium doneness. Allow to rest for 10 minutes before serving. Garnish with sprigs of oregano, rosemary, and thyme, and lavender flowers, if desired. Serve with lemon slices, if desired. Best served fresh. Store leftovers in an airtight container in the fridge for up to 4 days. Serve chilled over a salad, or reheat in a 175ºC air fryer for 3 minutes, or until heated through.

## Meat and Rice Stuffed Peppers

**Prep time: 20 minutes | Cook time: 18 minutes | Serves 4**

340 g lean beef mince
110 g lean pork mince
60 ml onion, minced
1 (425 g) can finely-chopped tomatoes
1 teaspoon Worcestershire sauce
1 teaspoon barbecue seasoning
1 teaspoon honey
½ teaspoon dried basil
120 ml cooked brown rice
½ teaspoon garlic powder
½ teaspoon oregano
½ teaspoon salt
2 small peppers, cut in half, stems removed, deseeded
Cooking spray

Preheat the air fryer to 180ºC and spritz a baking pan with cooking spray. Arrange the beef, pork, and onion in the baking pan and bake in the preheated air fryer for 8 minutes. Break the ground meat into chunks halfway through the cooking. Meanwhile, combine the tomatoes, Worcestershire sauce, barbecue seasoning, honey, and basil in a saucepan. Stir to mix well. Transfer the cooked meat mixture to a large bowl and add the cooked rice, garlic powder, oregano, salt, and 60 ml of the tomato mixture. Stir to mix well. Stuff the pepper halves with the mixture, then arrange the pepper halves in the air fryer and air fry for 10 minutes or until the peppers are lightly charred. Serve the stuffed peppers with the remaining tomato sauce on top.

## Currywurst

**Prep time: 15 minutes | Cook time: 12 minutes | Serves 4**

235 ml tomato sauce
2 tablespoons cider vinegar
2 teaspoons curry powder
2 teaspoons sweet paprika
1 teaspoon sugar

¼ teaspoon cayenne pepper
1 small onion, diced
450 g bratwurst, sliced
diagonally into 1-inch pieces

In a large bowl, combine the tomato sauce, vinegar, curry powder, paprika, sugar, and cayenne. Whisk until well combined. Stir in the onion and bratwurst. Transfer the mixture to a baking pan. Place the pan in the air fryer basket. Set the air fryer to 200°C for 12 minutes, or until the sausage is heated through and the sauce is bubbling.

## Asian Glazed Meatballs

**Prep time: 15 minutes | Cook time: 10 minutes per batch | Serves 4 to 6**

1 large shallot, finely chopped
2 cloves garlic, minced
1 tablespoon grated fresh ginger
2 teaspoons fresh thyme, finely chopped
355 ml brown mushrooms, very finely chopped (a food processor works well here)
2 tablespoons soy sauce
Freshly ground black pepper, to

taste
450 g beef mince
230 g pork mince
3 egg yolks
235 ml Thai sweet chili sauce (spring roll sauce)
60 ml toasted sesame seeds
2 spring onionspring onions, sliced

Combine the shallot, garlic, ginger, thyme, mushrooms, soy sauce, freshly ground black pepper, beef and pork mince, and egg yolks in a bowl and mix the ingredients together. Gently shape the mixture into 24 balls, about the size of a golf ball. Preheat the air fryer to 190°C. Working in batches, air fry the meatballs for 8 minutes, turning the meatballs over halfway through the cooking time. Drizzle some of the Thai sweet chili sauce on top of each meatball and return the basket to the air fryer, air frying for another 2 minutes. Reserve the remaining Thai sweet chili sauce for serving. As soon as the meatballs are done, sprinkle with toasted sesame seeds and transfer them to a serving platter. Scatter the spring onionspring onions around and serve warm.

## Sumptuous Pizza Tortilla Rolls

**Prep time: 10 minutes | Cook time: 6 minutes | Serves 4**

1 teaspoon butter
½ medium onion, slivered
½ red or green pepper, julienned
110 g fresh white mushrooms, chopped
120 ml pizza sauce

8 flour tortillas
8 thin slices wafer-thinham
24 pepperoni slices
235 ml shredded Mozzarella cheese
Cooking spray

Preheat the air fryer to 200°C. Put butter, onions, pepper, and mushrooms in a baking pan. Bake in the preheated air fryer for 3

minutes. Stir and cook 3 to 4 minutes longer until just crisp and tender. Remove pan and set aside. To assemble rolls, spread about 2 teaspoons of pizza sauce on one half of each tortilla. Top with a slice of ham and 3 slices of pepperoni. Divide sautéed vegetables among tortillas and top with cheese. Roll up tortillas, secure with toothpicks if needed, and spray with oil. Put 4 rolls in air fryer basket and air fry for 4 minutes. Turn and air fry 4 minutes, until heated through and lightly browned. Repeat step 4 to air fry remaining pizza rolls. Serve immediately.

## Air Fryer Chicken-Fried Steak

**Prep time: 5 minutes | Cook time: 20 minutes | Serves 4**

450 g beef braising steak
700 ml low-fat milk, divided
1 teaspoon dried thyme
1 teaspoon dried rosemary

2 medium egg whites
235 ml gluten-free breadcrumbs
120 ml coconut flour
1 tablespoon Cajun seasoning

In a bowl, marinate the steak in 475 ml of milk for 30 to 45 minutes. Remove the steak from milk, shake off the excess liquid, and season with the thyme and rosemary. Discard the milk. In a shallow bowl, beat the egg whites with the remaining 235 ml of milk. In a separate shallow bowl, combine the breadcrumbs, coconut flour, and seasoning. Dip the steak in the egg white mixture then dredge in the breadcrumb mixture, coating well. Place the steak in the basket of an air fryer. Set the air fryer to 200°C, close, and cook for 10 minutes. Open the air fryer, turn the steaks, close, and cook for 10 minutes. Let rest for 5 minutes.

## Mozzarella Stuffed Beef and Pork Meatballs

**Prep time: 15 minutes | Cook time: 12 minutes | Serves 4 to 6**

1 tablespoon olive oil
1 small onion, finely chopped
1 to 2 cloves garlic, minced
340 g beef mince
340 g pork mince
180 ml bread crumbs
60 ml grated Parmesan cheese
60 ml finely chopped fresh parsley

½ teaspoon dried oregano
1½ teaspoons salt
Freshly ground black pepper, to taste
2 eggs, lightly beaten
140 g low-moisture Mozzarella or other melting cheese, cut into 1-inch cubes

Preheat a skillet over medium-high heat. Add the oil and cook the onion and garlic until tender, but not browned. Transfer the onion and garlic to a large bowl and add the beef, pork, bread crumbs, Parmesan cheese, parsley, oregano, salt, pepper and eggs. Mix well until all the ingredients are combined. Divide the mixture into 12 evenly sized balls. Make one meatball at a time, by pressing a hole in the meatball mixture with the finger and pushing a piece of Mozzarella cheese into the hole. Mold the meat back into a ball, enclosing the cheese. Preheat the air fryer to 190°C. Working in two batches, transfer six of the meatballs to the air fryer basket and air fry for 12 minutes, shaking the basket and turning the meatballs twice during the cooking process. Repeat with the remaining 6 meatballs. Serve warm.

## Goat Cheese-Stuffed Bavette Steak

**Prep time: 10 minutes | Cook time: 14 minutes | Serves 6**

450 g bavette or skirt steak
1 tablespoon avocado oil
½ teaspoon sea salt
½ teaspoon garlic powder

¼ teaspoon freshly ground
black pepper
60 g goat cheese, crumbled
235 ml baby spinach, chopped

Place the steak in a large zip-top bag or between two pieces of plastic wrap. Using a meat mallet or heavy-bottomed skillet, pound the steak to an even ¼-inch thickness. Brush both sides of the steak with the avocado oil. Mix the salt, garlic powder, and pepper in a small dish. Sprinkle this mixture over both sides of the steak. Sprinkle the goat cheese over top, and top that with the spinach. Starting at one of the long sides, roll the steak up tightly. Tie the rolled steak with kitchen string at 3-inch intervals. Set the air fryer to 200°C. Place the steak roll-up in the air fryer basket. Air fry for 7 minutes. Flip the steak and cook for an additional 7 minutes, until an instant-read thermometer reads 50°C for medium-rare (adjust the cooking time for your desired doneness).

## Greek Lamb Rack

**Prep time: 5 minutes | Cook time: 10 minutes | Serves 4**

60 ml freshly squeezed lemon
juice
1 teaspoon oregano
2 teaspoons minced fresh
rosemary
1 teaspoon minced fresh thyme

2 tablespoons minced garlic
Salt and freshly ground black
pepper, to taste
2 to 4 tablespoons olive oil
1 lamb rib rack (7 to 8 ribs)

Preheat the air fryer to 180°C. In a small mixing bowl, combine the lemon juice, oregano, rosemary, thyme, garlic, salt, pepper, and olive oil and mix well. Rub the mixture over the lamb, covering all the meat. Put the rack of lamb in the air fryer. Roast for 10 minutes. Flip the rack halfway through. After 10 minutes, measure the internal temperature of the rack of lamb reaches at least 65°C. Serve immediately.

## Bacon-Wrapped Cheese Pork

**Prep time: 10 minutes | Cook time: 20 minutes | Serves 4**

4 (1-inch-thick) boneless pork
chops
2 (150 g) packages Boursin

cheese
8 slices thin-cut bacon

Spray the air fryer basket with avocado oil. Preheat the air fryer to 200°C. Place one of the chops on a cutting board. With a sharp knife held parallel to the cutting board, make a 1-inch-wide incision on the top edge of the chop. Carefully cut into the chop to form a large pocket, leaving a ½-inch border along the sides and bottom. Repeat with the other 3 chops. Snip the corner of a large resealable plastic bag to form a ¾-inch hole. Place the Boursin cheese in the bag and pipe the cheese into the pockets in the chops, dividing the cheese evenly among them. Wrap 2 slices of bacon around each chop and secure the ends with toothpicks. Place the bacon-wrapped chops in the air fryer basket and cook for 10 minutes, then flip the chops and cook for another 8 to 10 minutes, until the bacon is crisp, the chops are cooked through, and the internal temperature reaches 65°C. Store leftovers in an airtight container in the refrigerator for up to 3 days. Reheat in a preheated 200°C air fryer for 5 minutes, or until warmed through.

## Sausage and Pork Meatballs

**Prep time: 15 minutes | Cook time: 8 to 12 minutes | Serves 8**

1 large egg
1 teaspoon gelatin
450 g pork mince
230 g Italian-seasoned sausage,
casings removed, crumbled
80 ml Parmesan cheese
60 ml finely diced onion
1 tablespoon tomato paste

1 teaspoon minced garlic
1 teaspoon dried oregano
¼ teaspoon red pepper flakes
Sea salt and freshly ground
black pepper, to taste
Keto-friendly marinara sauce,
for serving

Beat the egg in a small bowl and sprinkle with the gelatin. Allow to sit for 5 minutes. In a large bowl, combine the pork mince, sausage, Parmesan, onion, tomato paste, garlic, oregano, and red pepper flakes. Season with salt and black pepper. Stir the gelatin mixture, then add it to the other ingredients and, using clean hands, mix to ensure that everything is well combined. Form into 1½-inch round meatballs. Set the air fryer to 200°C. Place the meatballs in the air fryer basket in a single layer, cooking in batches as needed. Air fry for 5 minutes. Flip and cook for 3 to 7 minutes more, or until an instant-read thermometer reads 70°C.

## Stuffed Beef Fillet with Feta Cheese

**Prep time: 10 minutes | Cook time: 10 minutes | Serves 4**

680 g beef fillet, pounded to ¼
inch thick
3 teaspoons sea salt
1 teaspoon ground black pepper
60 g creamy goat cheese

120 ml crumbled feta cheese
60 ml finely chopped onions
2 cloves garlic, minced
Cooking spray

Preheat the air fryer to 200°C. Spritz the air fryer basket with cooking spray. Unfold the beef on a clean work surface. Rub the salt and pepper all over the beef to season. Make the filling for the stuffed beef fillet: Combine the goat cheese, feta, onions, and garlic in a medium bowl. Stir until well blended. Spoon the mixture in the center of the fillet. Roll the fillet up tightly like rolling a burrito and use some kitchen twine to tie the fillet. Arrange the fillet in the air fryer basket and air fry for 10 minutes, flipping the fillet halfway through to ensure even cooking, or until an instant-read thermometer inserted in the center of the fillet registers 55°C for medium-rare. Transfer to a platter and serve immediately.

# Sausage-Stuffed Peppers

**Prep time: 15 minutes | Cook time: 28 to 30 minutes | Serves 6**

Avocado oil spray
230 g Italian-seasoned sausage, casings removed
120 ml chopped mushrooms
60 ml diced onion
1 teaspoon Italian seasoning

Sea salt and freshly ground black pepper, to taste
235 ml keto-friendly marinara sauce
3 peppers, halved and seeded
85 g low-moisture Mozzarella or other melting cheese, shredded

Spray a large skillet with oil and place it over medium-high heat. Add the sausage and cook for 5 minutes, breaking up the meat with a wooden spoon. Add the mushrooms, onion, and Italian seasoning, and season with salt and pepper. Cook for 5 minutes more. Stir in the marinara sauce and cook until heated through. Scoop the sausage filling into the pepper halves. Set the air fryer to 175°C. Arrange the peppers in a single layer in the air fryer basket, working in batches if necessary. Air fry for 15 minutes. Top the stuffed peppers with the cheese and air fry for 3 to 5 minutes more, until the cheese is melted and the peppers are tender.

# Teriyaki Rump Steak with Broccoli and Capsicum

**Prep time: 5 minutes | Cook time: 13 minutes | Serves 4**

230 g rump steak
80 ml teriyaki marinade
1½ teaspoons sesame oil
½ head broccoli, cut into florets

2 red peppers, sliced
Fine sea salt and ground black pepper, to taste
Cooking spray

Toss the rump steak in a large bowl with teriyaki marinade. Wrap the bowl in plastic and refrigerate to marinate for at least an hour. Preheat the air fryer to 200°C and spritz with cooking spray. Discard the marinade and transfer the steak in the preheated air fryer. Spritz with cooking spray. Air fry for 13 minutes or until well browned. Flip the steak halfway through. Meanwhile, heat the sesame oil in a nonstick skillet over medium heat. Add the broccoli and red pepper. Sprinkle with salt and ground black pepper. Sauté for 5 minutes or until the broccoli is tender. Transfer the air fried rump steak on a plate and top with the sautéed broccoli and pepper. Serve hot.

# Pigs in a Blanket

**Prep time: 10 minutes | Cook time: 7 minutes | Serves 2**

120 ml shredded Mozzarella cheese
2 tablespoons blanched finely ground almond flour
30 g full-fat cream cheese

2 (110 g) beef smoked sausage, cut in two
½ teaspoon sesame seeds

Place Mozzarella, almond flour, and cream cheese in a large microwave-safe bowl. Microwave for 45 seconds and stir until smooth. Roll dough into a ball and cut in half. Press each half out into a 4 × 5-inch rectangle. Roll one sausage up in each dough half and press seams closed. Sprinkle the top with sesame seeds. Place each wrapped sausage into the air fryer basket. Adjust the temperature to 200°C and air fry for 7 minutes. The outside will be golden when completely cooked. Serve immediately.

# Chapter 5 Fish and Seafood

## Rainbow Salmon Kebabs

**Prep time: 10 minutes | Cook time: 8 minutes | Serves 2**

170 g boneless, skinless salmon, cut into 1-inch cubes
¼ medium red onion, peeled and cut into 1-inch pieces
½ medium yellow bell pepper, seeded and cut into 1-inch pieces

½ medium courgette, trimmed and cut into ½-inch slices
1 tablespoon olive oil
½ teaspoon salt
¼ teaspoon ground black pepper

Using one (6-inch) skewer, skewer 1 piece salmon, then 1 piece onion, 1 piece bell pepper, and finally 1 piece courgette. Repeat this pattern with additional skewers to make four kebabs total. Drizzle with olive oil and sprinkle with salt and black pepper. Place kebabs into ungreased air fryer basket. Adjust the temperature to 200°C and air fry for 8 minutes, turning kebabs halfway through cooking. Salmon will easily flake and have an internal temperature of at least 65°C when done; vegetables will be tender. Serve warm.

## Garlic Lemon Scallops

**Prep time: 5 minutes | Cook time: 10 minutes | Serves 4**

4 tablespoons salted butter, melted
4 teaspoons peeled and finely minced garlic
½ small lemon, zested and juiced

8 sea scallops, 30 g each, cleaned and patted dry
¼ teaspoon salt
¼ teaspoon ground black pepper

In a small bowl, mix butter, garlic, lemon zest, and lemon juice. Place scallops in an ungreased round nonstick baking dish. Pour butter mixture over scallops, then sprinkle with salt and pepper. Place dish into air fryer basket. Adjust the temperature to 180°C and bake for 10 minutes. Scallops will be opaque and firm, and have an internal temperature of 55°C when done. Serve warm.

## Tuna Patties with Spicy Sriracha Sauce

**Prep time: 10 minutes | Cook time: 10 minutes | Serves 4**

2 (170 g) cans tuna packed in oil, drained
3 tablespoons almond flour
2 tablespoons mayonnaise
1 teaspoon dried dill
½ teaspoon onion powder

Pinch of salt and pepper
Spicy Sriracha Sauce:
60 g mayonnaise
1 tablespoon Sriracha sauce
1 teaspoon garlic powder

Preheat the air fryer to 190°C. Line the basket with baking paper.

In a large bowl, combine the tuna, almond flour, mayonnaise, dill, and onion powder. Season to taste with salt and freshly ground black pepper. Use a fork to stir, mashing with the back of the fork as necessary, until thoroughly combined. Use an ice cream scoop to form the tuna mixture patties. Place the patties in a single layer on the baking paper in the air fryer basket. Press lightly with the bottom of the scoop to flatten into a circle about ½ inch thick. Pausing halfway through the cooking time to turn the patties, air fry for 10 minutes until lightly browned. To make the Sriracha sauce: In a small bowl, combine the mayonnaise, Sriracha, and garlic powder. Serve the tuna patties topped with the Sriracha sauce.

## Scallops and Spinach with Cream Sauce

**Prep time: 5 minutes | Cook time: 10 minutes | Serves 2**

Vegetable oil spray
280 g frozen spinach, thawed and drained
8 jumbo sea scallops
Kosher or coarse sea salt, and black pepper, to taste

180 ml heavy cream
1 tablespoon tomato paste
1 tablespoon chopped fresh basil
1 teaspoon minced garlic

Spray a baking pan with vegetable oil spray. Spread the thawed spinach in an even layer in the bottom of the pan. Spray both sides of the scallops with vegetable oil spray. Season lightly with salt and pepper. Arrange the scallops on top of the spinach. In a small bowl, whisk together the cream, tomato paste, basil, garlic, ½ teaspoon salt, and ½ teaspoon pepper. Pour the sauce over the scallops and spinach. Place the pan in the air fryer basket. Set the air fryer to 175°C for 10 minutes. Use a meat thermometer to ensure the scallops have an internal temperature of 55°C.

## Tuna Melt

**Prep time: 3 minutes | Cook time: 10 minutes | Serves 1**

Olive or vegetable oil, for spraying
140 g can tuna, drained
1 tablespoon mayonnaise
¼ teaspoon garlic granules, plus

more for garnish
2 teaspoons unsalted butte
2 slices sandwich bread of choice
2 slices Cheddar cheese

Line the air fryer basket with baking paper and spray lightly with oil. In a medium bowl, mix together the tuna, mayonnaise, and garlic. Spread 1 teaspoon of butter on each slice of bread and place one slice butter-side down in the prepared basket. Top with a slice of cheese, the tuna mixture, another slice of cheese, and the other slice of bread, butter-side up. Air fry at 200°C for 5 minutes, flip, and cook for another 5 minutes, until browned and crispy. Sprinkle with additional garlic, before cutting in half and serving.

## Confetti Salmon Burgers

**Prep time: 10 minutes | Cook time: 12 minutes | Serves 4**

| | |
|---|---|
| 400 g cooked fresh or canned salmon, flaked with a fork | such as Old Bay |
| | ½ teaspoon kosher or coarse sea salt |
| 40 g minced spring onions, white and light green parts only | ½ teaspoon black pepper |
| 40 g minced red bell pepper | 1 egg, beaten |
| 40 g minced celery | 30 g fresh bread crumbs |
| 2 small lemons | Vegetable oil, for spraying |
| 1 teaspoon crab boil seasoning | |

In a large bowl, combine the salmon, vegetables, the zest and juice of 1 of the lemons, crab boil seasoning, salt, and pepper. Add the egg and bread crumbs and stir to combine. Form the mixture into 4 patties weighing approximately 140 g each. Chill until firm, about 15 minutes. Preheat the air fryer to 200ºC. Spray the salmon patties with oil on all sides and spray the air fryer basket to prevent sticking. Air fry for 12 minutes, flipping halfway through, until the burgers are browned and cooked through. Cut the remaining lemon into 4 wedges and serve with the burgers.

## Country Prawns

**Prep time: 10 minutes | Cook time: 15 to 20 minutes | Serves 4**

| | |
|---|---|
| 455 g large prawns, peeled and deveined, with tails on | pieces |
| | 1 red bell pepper, cut into chunks |
| 455 g smoked sausage, cut into thick slices | 1 tablespoon Old Bay seasoning |
| 2 corn cobs, quartered | 2 tablespoons olive oil |
| 1 courgette, cut into bite-sized | Cooking spray |

Preheat the air fryer to 200ºC. Spray the air fryer basket lightly with cooking spray. In a large bowl, mix the prawns, sausage, corn, courgette, bell pepper, and Old Bay seasoning, and toss to coat with the spices. Add the olive oil and toss again until evenly coated. Spread the mixture in the air fryer basket in a single layer. You will need to cook in batches. Air fry for 15 to 20 minutes, or until cooked through, shaking the basket every 5 minutes for even cooking. Serve immediately.

## Coconut Prawns

**Prep time: 5 minutes | Cook time: 6 minutes | Serves 2**

| | |
|---|---|
| 230 g medium prawns, peeled and deveined | ½ teaspoon Old Bay seasoning |
| 2 tablespoons salted butter, melted | 25 g desiccated, unsweetened coconut |

In a large bowl, toss the prawns in butter and Old Bay seasoning. Place shredded coconut in bowl. Coat each piece of prawns in the coconut and place into the air fryer basket. Adjust the temperature to 200ºC and air fry for 6 minutes. Gently turn the prawns halfway through the cooking time. Serve immediately.

## Coconut Cream Mackerel

**Prep time: 10 minutes | Cook time: 6 minutes | Serves 4**

| | |
|---|---|
| 900 g mackerel fillet | 1 teaspoon cumin seeds |
| 240 ml coconut cream | 1 garlic clove, peeled, chopped |
| 1 teaspoon ground coriander | |

Chop the mackerel roughly and sprinkle it with coconut cream, ground coriander, cumin seeds, and garlic. Then put the fish in the air fryer and cook at 200ºC for 6 minutes.

## Scallops Gratiné with Parmesan

**Prep time: 10 minutes | Cook time: 9 minutes | Serves 2**

| | |
|---|---|
| Scallops: | ½ teaspoon black pepper |
| 120 ml single cream | 455 g sea scallops |
| 45 g grated Parmesan cheese | Topping: |
| 235 g thinly sliced spring onions | 30 g panko bread crumbs |
| | 20 g grated Parmesan cheese |
| 5 g chopped fresh parsley | Vegetable oil spray |
| 3 cloves garlic, minced | For Serving: |
| ½ teaspoon kosher or coarse sea salt | Lemon wedges |
| | Crusty French bread (optional) |

For the scallops: In a baking pan, combine the single cream, cheese, spring onions, parsley, garlic, salt, and pepper. Stir in the scallops. For the topping: In a small bowl, combine the bread crumbs and cheese. Sprinkle evenly over the scallops. Spray the topping with vegetable oil spray. Place the pan in the air fryer basket. Set the air fryer to 165ºC for 6 minutes. Set the air fryer to 200ºC for 3 minutes until the topping has browned. To serve: Squeeze the lemon wedges over the gratin and serve with crusty French bread, if desired.

## Prawn Creole Casserole

**Prep time: 20 minutes | Cook time: 25 minutes | Serves 4**

| | |
|---|---|
| 360 g prawns, peeled and deveined | 1 tablespoon cornflour |
| | 1 teaspoon Creole seasoning |
| 50 g chopped celery | ¾ teaspoon salt |
| 50 g chopped onion | ½ teaspoon freshly ground black pepper |
| 50 g chopped green bell pepper | |
| 2 large eggs, beaten | 120 g shredded Cheddar cheese |
| 240 ml single cream | Cooking spray |
| 1 tablespoon butter, melted | |

In a medium bowl, stir together the prawns, celery, onion, and green pepper. In another medium bowl, whisk the eggs, single cream, butter, cornflour, Creole seasoning, salt, and pepper until blended. Stir the egg mixture into the prawn mixture. Add the cheese and stir to combine. Preheat the air fryer to 150ºC. Spritz a baking pan with oil. Transfer the prawn mixture to the prepared pan and place it in the air fryer basket. Bake for 25 minutes, stirring every 10 minutes, until a knife inserted into the center comes out clean. Serve immediately.

## Orange-Mustard Glazed Salmon

**Prep time: 10 minutes | Cook time: 10 minutes | Serves 2**

| | |
|---|---|
| 1 tablespoon orange marmalade | 2 (230 g) skin-on salmon fillets, |
| ¼ teaspoon grated orange zest | 1½ inches thick |
| plus 1 tablespoon juice | Salt and pepper, to taste |
| 2 teaspoons whole-grain | Vegetable oil spray |
| mustard | |

Preheat the air fryer to 200ºC. Make foil sling for air fryer basket by folding 1 long sheet of aluminum foil so it is 4 inches wide. Lay sheet of foil widthwise across basket, pressing foil into and up sides of basket. Fold excess foil as needed so that edges of foil are flush with top of basket. Lightly spray foil and basket with vegetable oil spray. Combine marmalade, orange zest and juice, and mustard in bowl. Pat salmon dry with paper towels and season with salt and pepper. Brush tops and sides of fillets evenly with glaze. Arrange fillets skin side down on sling in prepared basket, spaced evenly apart. Air fry salmon until center is still translucent when checked with the tip of a paring knife and registers 50ºC (for medium-rare), 10 to 14 minutes, using sling to rotate fillets halfway through cooking. Using the sling, carefully remove salmon from air fryer. Slide fish spatula along underside of fillets and transfer to individual serving plates, leaving skin behind. Serve.

## Italian Baked Cod

**Prep time: 5 minutes | Cook time: 12 minutes | Serves 4**

| | |
|---|---|
| 4 cod fillets, 170 g each | ¼ teaspoon salt |
| 2 tablespoons salted butter, | 120 ml tomato-based pasta |
| melted | sauce |
| 1 teaspoon Italian seasoning | |

Place cod into an ungreased round nonstick baking dish. Pour butter over cod and sprinkle with Italian seasoning and salt. Top with pasta sauce. Place dish into air fryer basket. Adjust the temperature to 175ºC and bake for 12 minutes. Fillets will be lightly browned, easily flake, and have an internal temperature of at least 65ºC when done. Serve warm.

## Tilapia Sandwiches with Tartar Sauce

**Prep time: 8 minutes | Cook time: 17 minutes | Serves 4**

| | |
|---|---|
| 160 g mayonnaise | 40 g plain flour |
| 2 tablespoons dried minced | 1 egg, lightly beaten |
| onion | 200 g panko bread crumbs |
| 1 dill pickle spear, finely | 2 teaspoons lemon pepper |
| chopped | 4 (170 g) tilapia fillets |
| 2 teaspoons pickle juice | Olive oil spray |
| ¼ teaspoon salt | 4 soft sub rolls |
| ⅛ teaspoon freshly ground | 4 lettuce leaves |
| black pepper | |

To make the tartar sauce, in a small bowl, whisk the mayonnaise, dried onion, pickle, pickle juice, salt, and pepper until blended. Refrigerate while you make the fish. Scoop the flour onto a plate; set aside. Put the beaten egg in a medium shallow bowl. On another plate, stir together the panko and lemon pepper. Insert the crisper plate into the basket and the basket into the unit. Preheat the unit to 200ºC. Dredge the tilapia fillets in the flour, in the egg, and press into the panko mixture to coat. Once the unit is preheated, spray the crisper plate with olive oil and place a baking paper liner into the basket. Place the prepared fillets on the liner in a single layer. Lightly spray the fillets with olive oil. cook for 8 minutes, remove the basket, carefully flip the fillets, and spray them with more olive oil. Reinsert the basket to resume cooking. When the cooking is complete, the fillets should be golden and crispy and a food thermometer should register 65ºC. Place each cooked fillet in a sub roll, top with a little bit of tartar sauce and lettuce, and serve.

## Fish Cakes

**Prep time: 30 minutes | Cook time: 10 to 12 minutes | Serves 4**

| | |
|---|---|
| 1 large russet potato, mashed | 50 g potato starch |
| 340 g cod or other white fish | 60 g panko breadcrumbs |
| Salt and pepper, to taste | 1 tablespoon fresh chopped |
| Olive or vegetable oil for | chives |
| misting or cooking spray | 2 tablespoons minced onion |
| 1 large egg | |

Peel potatoes, cut into cubes, and cook on stovetop till soft. Salt and pepper raw fish to taste. Mist with oil or cooking spray, and air fry at 180ºC for 6 to 8 minutes, until fish flakes easily. If fish is crowded, rearrange halfway through cooking to ensure all pieces cook evenly. Transfer fish to a plate and break apart to cool. Beat egg in a shallow dish. Place potato starch in another shallow dish, and panko crumbs in a third dish. When potatoes are done, drain in colander and rinse with cold water. In a large bowl, mash the potatoes and stir in the chives and onion. Add salt and pepper to taste, then stir in the fish. If needed, stir in a tablespoon of the beaten egg to help bind the mixture. Shape into 8 small, fat patties. Dust lightly with potato starch, dip in egg, and roll in panko crumbs. Spray both sides with oil or cooking spray. 1Air fry for 10 to 12 minutes, until golden brown and crispy.

## Blackened Red Snapper

**Prep time: 13 minutes | Cook time: 8 to 10 minutes | Serves 4**

| | |
|---|---|
| 1½ teaspoons black pepper | 4 red snapper fillet portions, |
| ¼ teaspoon thyme | skin on, 110 g each |
| ¼ teaspoon garlic powder | 4 thin slices lemon |
| ⅛ teaspoon cayenne pepper | Cooking spray |
| 1 teaspoon olive oil | |

Mix the spices and oil together to make a paste. Rub into both sides of the fish. Spray the air fryer basket with nonstick cooking spray and lay snapper steaks in basket, skin-side down. Place a lemon slice on each piece of fish. Roast at 200ºC for 8 to 10 minutes. The fish will not flake when done, but it should be white through the center.

## Salmon with Cauliflower

**Prep time: 10 minutes | Cook time: 25 minutes | Serves 4**

455 g salmon fillet, diced
100 g cauliflower, shredded
1 tablespoon dried coriander
1 tablespoon coconut oil,

melted
1 teaspoon ground turmeric
60 ml coconut cream

Mix salmon with cauliflower, dried cilantro, ground turmeric, coconut cream, and coconut oil. Transfer the salmon mixture into the air fryer and cook the meal at 175°C for 25 minutes. Stir the meal every 5 minutes to avoid the burning.

## Chinese Ginger-Spring Onion Fish

**Prep time: 15 minutes | Cook time: 15 minutes | Serves 2**

Bean Sauce:
2 tablespoons soy sauce
1 tablespoon rice wine
1 tablespoon doubanjiang
(Chinese black bean paste)
1 teaspoon minced fresh ginger
1 clove garlic, minced
Vegetables and Fish:
1 tablespoon peanut oil
235 g julienned spring onions
(white and green parts)
5 g chopped fresh coriander
2 tablespoons julienned fresh
ginger
2 (170) g white fish fillets, such
as tilapia

Bean Sauce:
2 tablespoons soy sauce
1 tablespoon rice wine
1 tablespoon doubanjiang
(Chinese black bean paste)
1 teaspoon minced fresh ginger
1 clove garlic, minced
Vegetables and Fish:
1 tablespoon peanut oil
235 g julienned spring onions
(white and green parts)
5 g chopped fresh coriander
2 tablespoons julienned fresh
ginger
2 (170 g) white fish fillets, such
as tilapia

For the sauce: In a small bowl, combine all the ingredients and stir until well combined; set aside. For the vegetables and fish: In a medium bowl, combine the peanut oil, spring onions, coriander, and ginger. Toss to combine. Cut two squares of baking paper large enough to hold one fillet and half of the vegetables. Place one fillet on each baking paper square, top with the vegetables, and pour over the sauce. Fold over the baking paper and crimp the sides in small, tight folds to hold the fish, vegetables, and sauce securely inside the packet. Place the packets in a single layer in the air fryer basket. Set fryer to 175°C for 15 minutes. Transfer each packet to a dinner plate. Cut open with scissors just before serving. For the sauce: In a small bowl, combine all the ingredients and stir until well combined; set aside. For the vegetables and fish: In a medium bowl, combine the peanut oil, spring onions, coriander, and ginger. Toss to combine. Cut two squares of baking paper large enough to hold one fillet and half of the vegetables. Place one fillet on each baking paper square, top with the vegetables, and pour over the sauce. Fold over the parchment paper and crimp the sides in small, tight folds to hold the fish, vegetables, and sauce securely inside the packet. Place the packets in a single layer in the air fryer basket. Cook for 15 minutes. Transfer each packet to a dinner plate. Cut open with scissors just before serving. For the sauce: In a small bowl, combine all the ingredients and stir until well combined; set aside. For the vegetables and fish: In a medium bowl, combine the peanut oil, spring onions, coriander, and ginger. Toss to combine.

Cut two squares of baking paper large enough to hold one fillet and half of the vegetables. Place one fillet on each baking paper square, top with the vegetables, and pour over the sauce. Fold over the baking paper and crimp the sides in small, tight folds to hold the fish, vegetables, and sauce securely inside the packet. Place the packets in a single layer in the air fryer basket. Keep fryer at 175°C and cook for 15 minutes. Transfer each packet to a dinner plate. Cut open with scissors just before serving.

## Herbed Prawns Pita

**Prep time: 5 minutes | Cook time: 8 minutes | Serves 4**

455 g medium prawns, peeled
and deveined
2 tablespoons olive oil
1 teaspoon dried oregano
½ teaspoon dried thyme
½ teaspoon garlic powder
¼ teaspoon onion powder
½ teaspoon salt

¼ teaspoon black pepper
4 whole wheat pitas
110 g feta cheese, crumbled
75 g shredded lettuce
1 tomato, diced
45 g black olives, sliced
1 lemon

Preheat the oven to 190°C. In a medium bowl, combine the prawns with the olive oil, oregano, thyme, garlic powder, onion powder, salt, and black pepper. Pour prawns in a single layer in the air fryer basket and roast for 6 to 8 minutes, or until cooked through. Remove from the air fryer and divide into warmed pitas with feta, lettuce, tomato, olives, and a squeeze of lemon.

## Sweet Tilapia Fillets

**Prep time: 5 minutes | Cook time: 14 minutes | Serves 4**

2 tablespoons granulated
sweetener
1 tablespoon apple cider

vinegar
4 tilapia fillets, boneless
1 teaspoon olive oil

Mix apple cider vinegar with olive oil and sweetener. Then rub the tilapia fillets with the sweet mixture and put in the air fryer basket in one layer. Cook the fish at 180°C for 7 minutes per side.

## Roasted Halibut Steaks with Parsley

**Prep time: 5 minutes | Cook time: 10 minutes | Serves 4**

455 g halibut steaks
60 ml vegetable oil
2½ tablespoons Worcester
sauce
2 tablespoons honey
2 tablespoons vermouth or
white wine vinegar

1 tablespoon freshly squeezed
lemon juice
1 tablespoon fresh parsley
leaves, coarsely chopped
Salt and pepper, to taste
1 teaspoon dried basil

Preheat the air fryer to 200°C. Put all the ingredients in a large mixing dish and gently stir until the fish is coated evenly. Transfer the fish to the air fryer basket and roast for 10 minutes, flipping the fish halfway through, or until the fish reaches an internal temperature of at least 65°C on a meat thermometer. Let the fish cool for 5 minutes and serve.

## Nutty Prawns with Amaretto Glaze

**Prep time: 30 minutes | Cook time: 10 minutes per batch | Serves 10 to 12**

| | |
|---|---|
| 120 g plain flour | oil |
| ½ teaspoon baking powder | 185 g sliced almonds |
| 1 teaspoon salt | 900 g large prawns (about |
| 2 eggs, beaten | 32 to 40 prawns), peeled and |
| 120 ml milk | deveined, tails left on |
| 2 tablespoons olive or vegetable | 470 ml amaretto liqueur |

Combine the flour, baking powder and salt in a large bowl. Add the eggs, milk and oil and stir until it forms a smooth batter. Coarsely crush the sliced almonds into a second shallow dish with your hands. Dry the prawns well with paper towels. Dip the prawns into the batter and shake off any excess batter, leaving just enough to lightly coat the prawns. Transfer the prawns to the dish with the almonds and coat completely. Place the coated prawns on a plate or baking sheet and when all the prawns have been coated, freeze the prawns for an 1 hour, or as long as a week before air frying. Preheat the air fryer to 200ºC. Transfer 8 frozen prawns at a time to the air fryer basket. Air fry for 6 minutes. Turn the prawns over and air fry for an additional 4 minutes. Repeat with the remaining prawns. While the prawns are cooking, bring the Amaretto to a boil in a small saucepan on the stovetop. Lower the heat and simmer until it has reduced and thickened into a glaze, about 10 minutes. Remove the prawns from the air fryer and brush both sides with the warm amaretto glaze. Serve warm.

## Lemon-Tarragon Fish en Papillote

**Prep time: 10 minutes | Cook time: 15 minutes | Serves 2**

| | |
|---|---|
| 2 tablespoons salted butter, melted | 435 g julienned fennel, or 1 stalk julienned celery |
| 1 tablespoon fresh lemon juice | 75 g thinly sliced red bell pepper |
| ½ teaspoon dried tarragon, crushed, or 2 sprigs fresh tarragon | 2 cod fillets, 170 g each, thawed if frozen |
| 1 teaspoon kosher or coarse sea salt | Vegetable oil spray |
| 85 g julienned carrots | ½ teaspoon black pepper |

In a medium bowl, combine the butter, lemon juice, tarragon, and ½ teaspoon of the salt. Whisk well until you get a creamy sauce. Add the carrots, fennel, and bell pepper and toss to combine; set aside. Cut two squares of baking paper each large enough to hold one fillet and half the vegetables. Spray the fillets with vegetable oil spray. Season both sides with the remaining ½ teaspoon salt and the black pepper. Lay one fillet down on each baking paper square. Top each with half the vegetables. Pour any remaining sauce over the vegetables. Fold over the baking paper and crimp the sides in small, tight folds to hold the fish, vegetables, and sauce securely inside the packet. Place the packets in the air fryer basket. Set the air fryer to 175ºC for 15 minutes. Transfer each packet to a plate. Cut open with scissors just before serving (be careful, as the steam inside will be hot).

## Oyster Po'Boy

**Prep time: 20 minutes | Cook time: 5 minutes | Serves 4**

| | |
|---|---|
| 105 g plain flour | 1 (12-inch) French baguette, |
| 40 g yellow cornmeal | quartered and sliced |
| 1 tablespoon Cajun seasoning | horizontally |
| 1 teaspoon salt | Tartar Sauce, as needed |
| 2 large eggs, beaten | 150 g shredded lettuce, divided |
| 1 teaspoon hot sauce | 2 tomatoes, cut into slices |
| 455 g pre-shucked oysters | Cooking spray |

In a shallow bowl, whisk the flour, cornmeal, Cajun seasoning, and salt until blended. In a second shallow bowl, whisk together the eggs and hot sauce. One at a time, dip the oysters in the cornmeal mixture, the eggs, and again in the cornmeal, coating thoroughly. Preheat the air fryer to 200ºC. Line the air fryer basket with baking paper. Place the oysters on the baking paper and spritz with oil. Air fry for 2 minutes. Shake the basket, spritz the oysters with oil, and air fry for 3 minutes more until lightly browned and crispy. Spread each sandwich half with Tartar Sauce. Assemble the po'boys by layering each sandwich with fried oysters, ½ cup shredded lettuce, and 2 tomato slices. Serve immediately.

## Cod with Jalapeño

**Prep time: 5 minutes | Cook time: 14 minutes | Serves 4**

| | |
|---|---|
| 4 cod fillets, boneless | 1 tablespoon avocado oil |
| 1 jalapeño, minced | ½ teaspoon minced garlic |

In the shallow bowl, mix minced jalapeño, avocado oil, and minced garlic. Put the cod fillets in the air fryer basket in one layer and top with minced jalapeño mixture. Cook the fish at 185ºC for 7 minutes per side.

## Lemony Prawns and Courgette

**Prep time: 15 minutes | Cook time: 7 to 8 minutes | Serves 4**

| | |
|---|---|
| 570 g extra-large raw prawns, peeled and deveined | 1½ teaspoons dried oregano |
| 2 medium courgettes (about 230 g each), halved lengthwise and cut into ½-inch-thick slices | ⅛ teaspoon crushed red pepper flakes (optional) |
| 1½ tablespoons olive oil | Juice of ½ lemon |
| ½ teaspoon garlic salt | 1 tablespoon chopped fresh mint |
| | 1 tablespoon chopped fresh dill |

Preheat the air fryer to 175ºC. In a large bowl, combine the prawns, courgette, oil, garlic salt, oregano, and pepper flakes (if using) and toss to coat. Working in batches, arrange a single layer of the prawns and courgette in the air fryer basket. Air fry for 7 to 8 minutes, shaking the basket halfway, until the courgette is golden and the prawns are cooked through. Transfer to a serving dish and tent with foil while you air fry the remaining prawns and courgette. Top with the lemon juice, mint, and dill and serve.

# Prawns Curry

**Prep time: 30 minutes | Cook time: 10 minutes | Serves 4**

180 ml unsweetened full-fat coconut milk
10 g finely chopped yellow onion
2 teaspoons garam masala
1 tablespoon minced fresh ginger
1 tablespoon minced garlic

1 teaspoon ground turmeric
1 teaspoon salt
¼ to ½ teaspoon cayenne pepper
455 g raw prawns (21 to 25 count), peeled and deveined
2 teaspoons chopped fresh coriander

In a large bowl, stir together the coconut milk, onion, garam masala, ginger, garlic, turmeric, salt and cayenne, until well blended. Add the prawns and toss until coated with sauce on all sides. Marinate at room temperature for 30 minutes. Transfer the prawns and marinade to a baking pan. Place the pan in the air fryer basket. Set the air fryer to 190ºC for 10 minutes, stirring halfway through the cooking time. Transfer the prawns to a serving bowl or platter. Sprinkle with the cilantro and serve.

# Snapper Scampi

**Prep time: 5 minutes | Cook time: 8 to 10 minutes | Serves 4**

4 skinless snapper or arctic char fillets, 170 g each
1 tablespoon olive oil
3 tablespoons lemon juice, divided
½ teaspoon dried basil

Pinch salt
Freshly ground black pepper, to taste
2 tablespoons butter
2 cloves garlic, minced

Rub the fish fillets with olive oil and 1 tablespoon of the lemon juice. Sprinkle with the basil, salt, and pepper, and place in the air fryer basket. Air fry the fish at 190ºC for 7 to 8 minutes or until the fish just flakes when tested with a fork. Remove the fish from the basket and put on a serving plate. Cover to keep warm. In a baking pan, combine the butter, remaining 2 tablespoons lemon juice, and garlic. Bake in the air fryer for 1 to 2 minutes or until the garlic is sizzling. Pour this mixture over the fish and serve

# Pecan-Crusted Catfish

**Prep time: 5 minutes | Cook time: 12 minutes | Serves 4**

65 g pecans, finely crushed
1 teaspoon fine sea salt
¼ teaspoon ground black pepper

4 catfish fillets, 110g each
For Garnish (Optional):
Fresh oregano
Pecan halves

Spray the air fryer basket with avocado oil. Preheat the air fryer to 190ºC. In a large bowl, mix the crushed pecan, salt, and pepper. One at a time, dredge the catfish fillets in the mixture, coating them well. Use your hands to press the pecan meal into the fillets. Spray the fish with avocado oil and place them in the air fryer basket. Air fry the coated catfish for 12 minutes, or until it flakes easily and

is no longer translucent in the center, flipping halfway through. Garnish with oregano sprigs and pecan halves, if desired. Store leftovers in an airtight container in the fridge for up to 3 days. Reheat in a preheated 175ºC air fryer for 4 minutes, or until heated through.

# Chilean Sea Bass with Olive Relish

**Prep time: 10 minutes | Cook time: 10 minutes | Serves 2**

Olive oil spray
2 (170 g) Chilean sea bass fillets or other firm-fleshed white fish
3 tablespoons extra-virgin olive oil
½ teaspoon ground cumin

½ teaspoon kosher or coarse sea salt
½ teaspoon black pepper
60 g pitted green olives, diced
10 g finely diced onion
1 teaspoon chopped capers

Spray the air fryer basket with the olive oil spray. Drizzle the fillets with the olive oil and sprinkle with the cumin, salt, and pepper. Place the fish in the air fryer basket. Set the air fryer to 165ºC for 10 minutes, or until the fish flakes easily with a fork. Meanwhile, in a small bowl, stir together the olives, onion, and capers. Serve the fish topped with the relish.

# Butter-Wine Baked Salmon

**Prep time: 5 minutes | Cook time: 10 minutes | Serves 4**

4 tablespoons butter, melted
2 cloves garlic, minced
Sea salt and ground black pepper, to taste
60 ml dry white wine or apple cider vinegar

1 tablespoon lime juice
1 teaspoon smoked paprika
½ teaspoon onion powder
4 salmon steaks
Cooking spray

Place all the ingredients except the salmon and oil in a shallow dish and stir to mix well. Add the salmon steaks, turning to coat well on both sides. Transfer the salmon to the refrigerator to marinate for 30 minutes. Preheat the air fryer to 180ºC. Place the salmon steaks in the air fryer basket, discarding any excess marinade. Spray the salmon steaks with cooking spray. Air fry for about 10 minutes, flipping the salmon steaks halfway through, or until cooked to your preferred doneness. Divide the salmon steaks among four plates and serve.

# Parmesan Mackerel with Coriander

**Prep time: 10 minutes | Cook time: 7 minutes | Serves 2**

340 g mackerel fillet
60 g Parmesan, grated

1 teaspoon ground coriander
1 tablespoon olive oil

Sprinkle the mackerel fillet with olive oil and put it in the air fryer basket. Top the fish with ground coriander and Parmesan. Cook the fish at 200ºC for 7 minutes.

## Cod with Avocado

**Prep time: 30 minutes | Cook time: 10 minutes | Serves 2**

90 g shredded cabbage
60 ml full-fat sour cream
2 tablespoons full-fat mayonnaise
20 g chopped pickled jalapeños
2 (85 g) cod fillets
1 teaspoon chilli powder
1 teaspoon cumin
½ teaspoon paprika
¼ teaspoon garlic powder
1 medium avocado, peeled, pitted, and sliced
½ medium lime

In a large bowl, place cabbage, sour cream, mayonnaise, and jalapeños. Mix until fully coated. Let sit for 20 minutes in the refrigerator. Sprinkle cod fillets with chilli powder, cumin, paprika, and garlic powder. Place each fillet into the air fryer basket. Adjust the temperature to 190°C and set the timer for 10 minutes. Flip the fillets halfway through the cooking time. When fully cooked, fish should have an internal temperature of at least 65°C. To serve, divide slaw mixture into two serving bowls, break cod fillets into pieces and spread over the bowls, and top with avocado. Squeeze lime juice over each bowl. Serve immediately.

## Snapper with Shallot and Tomato

**Prep time: 20 minutes | Cook time: 15 minutes | Serves 2**

2 snapper fillets
1 shallot, peeled and sliced
2 garlic cloves, halved
1 bell pepper, sliced
1 small-sized serrano pepper, sliced
1 tomato, sliced
1 tablespoon olive oil
¼ teaspoon freshly ground black pepper
½ teaspoon paprika
Sea salt, to taste
2 bay leaves

Place two baking paper sheets on a working surface. Place the fish in the center of one side of the baking paper. Top with the shallot, garlic, peppers, and tomato. Drizzle olive oil over the fish and vegetables. Season with black pepper, paprika, and salt. Add the bay leaves. Fold over the other half of the baking paper. Now, fold the paper around the edges tightly and create a half moon shape, sealing the fish inside. Cook in the preheated air fryer at 200°C for 15 minutes. Serve warm.

## Steamed Cod with Garlic and Swiss Chard

**Prep time: 5 minutes | Cook time: 12 minutes | Serves 4**

1 teaspoon salt
½ teaspoon dried oregano
½ teaspoon dried thyme
½ teaspoon garlic powder
4 cod fillets
½ white onion, thinly sliced
135 g Swiss chard, washed, stemmed, and torn into pieces
60 ml olive oil
1 lemon, quartered

Preheat the air fryer to 190°C. In a small bowl, whisk together the salt, oregano, thyme, and garlic powder. Tear off four pieces of aluminum foil, with each sheet being large enough to envelop one cod fillet and a quarter of the vegetables. Place a cod fillet in the middle of each sheet of foil, then sprinkle on all sides with the spice mixture. In each foil packet, place a quarter of the onion slices and 30 g Swiss chard, then drizzle 1 tablespoon olive oil and squeeze ¼ lemon over the contents of each foil packet. Fold and seal the sides of the foil packets and then place them into the air fryer basket. Steam for 12 minutes. Remove from the basket, and carefully open each packet to avoid a steam burn.

## Classic Fish Sticks with Tartar Sauce

**Prep time: 10 minutes | Cook time: 12 to 15 minutes | Serves 4**

680 g cod fillets, cut into 1-inch strips
1 teaspoon salt
½ teaspoon freshly ground black pepper
2 eggs
70 g almond flour
20 g grated Parmesan cheese
Tartar Sauce:
120 ml sour cream
120 ml mayonnaise
3 tablespoons chopped dill pickle
2 tablespoons capers, drained and chopped
½ teaspoon dried dill
1 tablespoon dill pickle liquid (optional)

Preheat the air fryer to 200°C. Season the cod with the salt and black pepper; set aside. In a shallow bowl, lightly beat the eggs. In a second shallow bowl, combine the almond flour and Parmesan cheese. Stir until thoroughly combined. Working with a few pieces at a time, dip the fish into the egg mixture followed by the flour mixture. Press lightly to ensure an even coating. Working in batches if necessary, arrange the fish in a single layer in the air fryer basket and spray lightly with olive oil. Pausing halfway through the cooking time to turn the fish, air fry for 12 to 15 minutes, until the fish flakes easily with a fork. Let sit in the basket for a few minutes before serving with the tartar sauce. To make the tartar sauce: In a small bowl, combine the sour cream, mayonnaise, pickle, capers, and dill. If you prefer a thinner sauce, stir in the pickle liquid.

## Garlic Butter Prawns Scampi

**Prep time: 5 minutes | Cook time: 8 minutes | Serves 4**

Sauce:
60 g unsalted butter
2 tablespoons fish stock or chicken broth
2 cloves garlic, minced
2 tablespoons chopped fresh basil leaves
1 tablespoon lemon juice
1 tablespoon chopped fresh parsley, plus more for garnish
1 teaspoon red pepper flakes
Prawns:
455 g large prawns, peeled and deveined, tails removed
Fresh basil sprigs, for garnish

Preheat the air fryer to 175°C. Put all the ingredients for the sauce in a baking pan and stir to incorporate. Transfer the baking pan to the air fryer and air fry for 3 minutes, or until the sauce is heated through. Once done, add the prawns to the baking pan, flipping to coat in the sauce. Return to the air fryer and cook for another 5 minutes, or until the prawns are pink and opaque. Stir the prawns twice during cooking. Serve garnished with the parsley and basil sprigs.

## Garlic Prawns

**Prep time: 15 minutes | Cook time: 10 minutes | Serves 3**

Prawns:
Olive or vegetable oil, for spraying
450 g medium raw prawns, peeled and deveined
6 tablespoons unsalted butter, melted
120 g panko bread crumbs
2 tablespoons garlic granules

1 teaspoon salt
½ teaspoon freshly ground black pepper
Garlic Butter Sauce:
115 g unsalted butter
2 teaspoons garlic granules
¾ teaspoon salt (omit if using salted butter)

Make the Prawns Preheat the air fryer to 200°C. Line the air fryer basket with baking paper and spray lightly with oil. Place the prawns and melted butter in a zip-top plastic bag, seal, and shake well, until evenly coated. In a medium bowl, mix together the breadcrumbs, garlic, salt, and black pepper. Add the prawns to the panko mixture and toss until evenly coated. Shake off any excess coating. Place the prawns in the prepared basket and spray lightly with oil. Cook for 8 to 10 minutes, flipping and spraying with oil after 4 to 5 minutes, until golden brown and crispy. Make the Garlic Butter Sauce In a microwave-safe bowl, combine the butter, garlic, and salt and microwave on 50% power for 30 to 60 seconds, stirring every 15 seconds, until completely melted. Serve the prawns immediately with the garlic butter sauce on the side for dipping.

## Thai Prawn Skewers with Peanut Dipping Sauce

**Prep time: 15 minutes | Cook time: 6 minutes | Serves 2**

Salt and pepper, to taste
340 g extra-large prawns, peeled and deveined
1 tablespoon vegetable oil
1 teaspoon honey
½ teaspoon grated lime zest plus 1 tablespoon juice, plus lime wedges for serving

6 (6-inch) wooden skewers
3 tablespoons creamy peanut butter
3 tablespoons hot tap water
1 tablespoon chopped fresh coriander
1 teaspoon fish sauce

Preheat the air fryer to 200°C. Dissolve 2 tablespoons salt in 1 litre cold water in a large container. Add prawns, cover, and refrigerate for 15 minutes. Remove prawns from brine and pat dry with paper towels. Whisk oil, honey, lime zest, and ¼ teaspoon pepper together in a large bowl. Add prawns and toss to coat. Thread prawns onto skewers, leaving about ¼ inch between each prawns (3 or 4 prawns per skewer). Arrange 3 skewers in air fryer basket, parallel to each other and spaced evenly apart. Arrange remaining 3 skewers on top, perpendicular to the bottom layer. Air fry until prawns are opaque throughout, 6 to 8 minutes, flipping and rotating skewers halfway through cooking. Whisk peanut butter, hot tap water, lime juice, coriander, and fish sauce together in a bowl until smooth. Serve skewers with peanut dipping sauce and lime wedges.

## Fish Fillets with Lemon-Dill Sauce

**Prep time: 5 minutes | Cook time: 7 minutes | Serves 4**

455 g snapper, grouper, or salmon fillets
Sea salt and freshly ground black pepper, to taste
1 tablespoon avocado oil
60 g sour cream

60 g mayonnaise
2 tablespoons fresh dill, chopped, plus more for garnish
1 tablespoon freshly squeezed lemon juice
½ teaspoon grated lemon zest

Pat the fish dry with paper towels and season well with salt and pepper. Brush with the avocado oil. Set the air fryer to 200°C. Place the fillets in the air fryer basket and air fry for 1 minute. Lower the air fryer temperature to 165°C and continue cooking for 5 minutes. Flip the fish and cook for 1 minute more or until an instant-read thermometer reads 65°C. (If using salmon, cook it to 50°C /125°F for medium-rare.) While the fish is cooking, make the sauce by combining the sour cream, mayonnaise, dill, lemon juice, and lemon zest in a medium bowl. Season with salt and pepper and stir until combined. Refrigerate until ready to serve. Serve the fish with the sauce, garnished with the remaining dill.

# Chapter 6 Fast and Easy Everyday Favourites

## Baked Halloumi with Greek Salsa

### Prep timeBaked Halloumi with Greek Salsa

Salsa:
1 small shallot, finely diced
3 garlic cloves, minced
2 tablespoons fresh lemon juice
2 tablespoons extra-virgin olive oil
1 teaspoon freshly cracked black pepper
Pinch of rock salt
120 ml finely diced English cucumber
1 plum tomato, deseeded and

finely diced
2 teaspoons chopped fresh parsley
1 teaspoon snipped fresh dill
1 teaspoon snipped fresh oregano
Cheese:
227 g Halloumi cheese, sliced into ½-inch-thick pieces
1 tablespoon extra-virgin olive oil

Preheat the air fryer to 190°C. For the salsa: Combine the shallot, garlic, lemon juice, olive oil, pepper, and salt in a medium bowl. Add the cucumber, tomato, parsley, dill, and oregano. Toss gently to combine; set aside. For the cheese: Place the cheese slices in a medium bowl. Drizzle with the olive oil. Toss gently to coat. Arrange the cheese in a single layer in the air fryer basket. Bake for 6 minutes. Divide the cheese among four serving plates. Top with the salsa and serve immediately.

## Simple and Easy Croutons

### Prep time: 5 minutes | Cook time: 8 minutes | Serves 4

2 slices bread
1 tablespoon olive oil

Hot soup, for serving

Preheat the air fryer to 200°C. Cut the slices of bread into medium-size chunks. Brush the air fryer basket with the oil. Place the chunks inside and air fry for at least 8 minutes. Serve with hot soup.

## Rosemary and Orange Roasted Chickpeas

### Prep time: 5 minutes | Cook time: 10 to 12 minutes | Makes 1 L

1 L cooked chickpeas
2 tablespoons vegetable oil
1 teaspoon rock salt
1 teaspoon cumin

1 teaspoon paprika
Zest of 1 orange
1 tablespoon chopped fresh rosemary

Preheat the air fryer to 200°C. Make sure the chickpeas are completely dry prior to roasting. In a medium bowl, toss the chickpeas with oil, salt, cumin, and paprika. Working in batches, spread the chickpeas in a single layer in the air fryer basket. Air fry for 10 to 12 minutes until crisp, shaking once halfway through. Return the warm chickpeas to the bowl and toss with the orange zest and rosemary. Allow to cool completely. Serve.

## Peppery Brown Rice Fritters

### Prep time: 10 minutes | Cook time: 8 to 10 minutes | Serves 4

1 (284 g) bag frozen cooked brown rice, thawed
1 egg
3 tablespoons brown rice flour
80 ml finely grated carrots
80 ml minced red pepper

2 tablespoons minced fresh basil
3 tablespoons grated Parmesan cheese
2 teaspoons olive oil

Preheat the air fryer to 190°C. In a small bowl, combine the thawed rice, egg, and flour and mix to blend. Stir in the carrots, pepper, basil, and Parmesan cheese. Form the mixture into 8 fritters and drizzle with the olive oil. Put the fritters carefully into the air fryer basket. Air fry for 8 to 10 minutes, or until the fritters are golden brown and cooked through. Serve immediately.

## Beery and Crunchy Onion Rings

### Prep time: 10 minutes | Cook time: 16 minutes | Serves 2 to 4

160 ml plain flour
1 teaspoon paprika
½ teaspoon bicarbonate of soda
1 teaspoon salt
½ teaspoon freshly ground black pepper
1 egg, beaten

180 ml beer
350 ml breadcrumbs
1 tablespoons olive oil
1 large Vidalia or sweet onion, peeled and sliced into ½-inch rings
Cooking spray

Preheat the air fryer to 180°C. Spritz the air fryer basket with cooking spray. Combine the flour, paprika, bicarbonate of soda, salt, and ground black pepper in a bowl. Stir to mix well. Combine the egg and beer in a separate bowl. Stir to mix well. Make a well in the centre of the flour mixture, then pour the egg mixture in the well. Stir to mix everything well. Pour the breadcrumbs and olive oil in a shallow plate. Stir to mix well. Dredge the onion rings gently into the flour and egg mixture, then shake the excess off and put into the plate of breadcrumbs. Flip to coat both sides well. Arrange the onion rings in the preheated air fryer. Air fry in batches for 16 minutes or until golden brown and crunchy. Flip the rings and put the bottom rings to the top halfway through. Serve immediately.

## Cheesy Potato Patties

### Prep time: 5 minutes | Cook time: 10 minutes | Serves 8

| | |
|---|---|
| 900 g white potatoes | ½ teaspoon hot paprika |
| 120 ml finely chopped spring onions | 475 ml shredded Colby or Monterey Jack cheese |
| ½ teaspoon freshly ground black pepper, or more to taste | 60 ml rapeseed oil |
| 1 tablespoon fine sea salt | 235 ml crushed crackers |

Preheat the air fryer to 180°C. Boil the potatoes until soft. Dry them off and peel them before mashing thoroughly, leaving no lumps. Combine the mashed potatoes with spring onions, pepper, salt, paprika, and cheese. Mould the mixture into balls with your hands and press with your palm to flatten them into patties. In a shallow dish, combine the rapeseed oil and crushed crackers. Coat the patties in the crumb mixture. Bake the patties for about 10 minutes, in multiple batches if necessary. Serve hot.

## Traditional Queso Fundido

### Prep time: 10 minutes | Cook time: 25 minutes | Serves 4

| | |
|---|---|
| 110 g fresh Mexican (or Spanish if unavailable) chorizo, casings removed | 475 ml shredded Oaxaca or Mozzarella cheese |
| 1 medium onion, chopped | 120 ml half-and-half (60 ml whole milk and 60 ml cream combined) |
| 3 cloves garlic, minced | |
| 235 ml chopped tomato | Celery sticks or tortilla chips, for serving |
| 2 jalapeños, deseeded and diced | |
| 2 teaspoons ground cumin | |

Preheat the air fryer to 200°C. In a baking pan, combine the chorizo, onion, garlic, tomato, jalapeños, and cumin. Stir to combine. Place the pan in the air fryer basket. Air fry for 15 minutes, or until the sausage is cooked, stirring halfway through the cooking time to break up the sausage. Add the cheese and half-and-half; stir to combine. Air fry for 10 minutes, or until the cheese has melted. Serve with celery sticks or tortilla chips.

## Air Fried Shishito Peppers

### Prep time: 5 minutes | Cook time: 5 minutes | Serves 4

| | |
|---|---|
| 230 g shishito or Padron peppers (about 24) | Coarse sea salt, to taste |
| 1 tablespoon olive oil | Lemon wedges, for serving |
| | Cooking spray |

Preheat the air fryer to 200°C. Spritz the air fryer basket with cooking spray. Toss the peppers with olive oil in a large bowl to coat well. Arrange the peppers in the preheated air fryer. Air fryer for 5 minutes or until blistered and lightly charred. Shake the basket and sprinkle the peppers with salt halfway through the cooking time. Transfer the peppers onto a plate and squeeze the lemon wedges on top before serving.

## Beetroot Salad with Lemon Vinaigrette

### Prep time: 10 minutes | Cook time: 12 to 15 minutes | Serves 4

| | |
|---|---|
| 6 medium red and golden beetroots, peeled and sliced | Cooking spray |
| | Vinaigrette: |
| 1 teaspoon olive oil | 2 teaspoons olive oil |
| ¼ teaspoon rock salt | 2 tablespoons chopped fresh chives |
| 120 ml crumbled feta cheese | |
| 2 L mixed greens | Juice of 1 lemon |

Preheat the air fryer to 180°C. In a large bowl, toss the beetroots, olive oil, and rock salt. Spray the air fryer basket with cooking spray, then place the beetroots in the basket and air fry for 12 to 15 minutes or until tender. While the beetroots cook, make the vinaigrette in a large bowl by whisking together the olive oil, lemon juice, and chives. Remove the beetroots from the air fryer, toss in the vinaigrette, and allow to cool for 5 minutes. Add the feta and serve on top of the mixed greens.

## Cheesy Jalapeño Cornbread

### Prep timeCheesy Jalapeño Cornbread

| | |
|---|---|
| 160 ml cornmeal | 180 ml whole milk |
| 80 ml plain flour | 1 large egg, beaten |
| ¾ teaspoon baking powder | 1 jalapeño pepper, thinly sliced |
| 2 tablespoons margarine, melted | 80 ml shredded extra mature Cheddar cheese |
| ½ teaspoon rock salt | Cooking spray |
| 1 tablespoon granulated sugar | |

Preheat the air fryer to 150°C. Spritz the air fryer basket with cooking spray. Combine all the ingredients in a large bowl. Stir to mix well. Pour the mixture in a baking pan. Arrange the pan in the preheated air fryer. Bake for 20 minutes or until a toothpick inserted in the centre of the bread comes out clean. When the cooking is complete, remove the baking pan from the air fryer and allow the bread to cool for a few minutes before slicing to serve.

## Cheesy Chilli Toast

### Prep time: 5 minutes | Cook time: 5 minutes | Serves 1

| | |
|---|---|
| 2 tablespoons grated Parmesan cheese | room temperature |
| | 10 to 15 thin slices serrano |
| 2 tablespoons grated Mozzarella cheese | chilli or jalapeño |
| | 2 slices sourdough bread |
| 2 teaspoons salted butter, at | ½ teaspoon black pepper |

Preheat the air fryer to 165°C. In a small bowl, stir together the Parmesan, Mozzarella, butter, and chillies. Spread half the mixture onto one side of each slice of bread. Sprinkle with the pepper. Place the slices, cheese-side up, in the air fryer basket. Bake for 5 minutes, or until the cheese has melted and started to brown slightly. Serve immediately.

## Cheesy Baked Grits

**Prep time: 10 minutes | Cook time: 12 minutes | Serves 6**

180 ml hot water
2 (28 g) packages instant grits
1 large egg, beaten
1 tablespoon butter, melted
2 cloves garlic, minced

½ to 1 teaspoon red pepper flakes
235 ml shredded Cheddar cheese or jalapeño Jack cheese

Preheat the air fryer to 200ºC. In a baking pan, combine the water, grits, egg, butter, garlic, and red pepper flakes. Stir until well combined. Stir in the shredded cheese. Place the pan in the air fryer basket and air fry for 12 minutes, or until the grits have cooked through and a knife inserted near the centre comes out clean. Let stand for 5 minutes before serving.

## Purple Potato Chips with Rosemary

**Prep time: 10 minutes | Cook time: 9 to 14 minutes | Serves 6**

235 ml Greek yoghurt
2 chipotle chillies, minced
2 tablespoons adobo or chipotle sauce
1 teaspoon paprika
1 tablespoon lemon juice
10 purple fingerling or

miniature potatoes
1 teaspoon olive oil
2 teaspoons minced fresh rosemary leaves
⅛ teaspoon cayenne pepper
¼ teaspoon coarse sea salt

Preheat the air fryer to 200ºC. In a medium bowl, combine the yoghurt, minced chillies, adobo sauce, paprika, and lemon juice. Mix well and refrigerate. Wash the potatoes and dry them with paper towels. Slice the potatoes lengthwise, as thinly as possible. You can use a mandoline, a vegetable peeler, or a very sharp knife. Combine the potato slices in a medium bowl and drizzle with the olive oil; toss to coat. Air fry the chips, in batches, in the air fryer basket, for 9 to 14 minutes. Use tongs to gently rearrange the chips halfway during cooking time. Sprinkle the chips with the rosemary, cayenne pepper, and sea salt. Serve with the chipotle sauce for dipping.

## Herb-Roasted Veggies

**Prep time: 10 minutes | Cook time: 14 to 18 minutes | Serves 4**

1 red pepper, sliced
1 (230 g) package sliced mushrooms
235 ml green beans, cut into 2-inch pieces

80 ml diced red onion
3 garlic cloves, sliced
1 teaspoon olive oil
½ teaspoon dried basil
½ teaspoon dried tarragon

Preheat the air fryer to 175ºC. In a medium bowl, mix the red pepper, mushrooms, green beans, red onion, and garlic. Drizzle with the olive oil. Toss to coat. Add the herbs and toss again. Place the vegetables in the air fryer basket. Roast for 14 to 18 minutes, or until tender. Serve immediately.

## Corn Fritters

**Prep time: 15 minutes | Cook time: 8 minutes | Serves 6**

235 ml self-raising flour
1 tablespoon sugar
1 teaspoon salt
1 large egg, lightly beaten

60 ml buttermilk
180 ml corn kernels
60 ml minced onion
Cooking spray

Preheat the air fryer to 175ºC. Line the air fryer basket with parchment paper. In a medium bowl, whisk the flour, sugar, and salt until blended. Stir in the egg and buttermilk. Add the corn and minced onion. Mix well. Shape the corn fritter batter into 12 balls. Place the fritters on the parchment and spritz with oil. Bake for 4 minutes. Flip the fritters, spritz them with oil, and bake for 4 minutes more until firm and lightly browned. Serve immediately.

## Crunchy Fried Okra

**Prep time: 5 minutes | Cook time: 8 to 10 minutes | Serves 4**

235 ml self-raising yellow cornmeal (alternatively add 1 tablespoon baking powder to cornmeal)
1 teaspoon Italian-style seasoning
1 teaspoon paprika

1 teaspoon salt
½ teaspoon freshly ground black pepper
2 large eggs, beaten
475 ml okra slices
Cooking spray

Preheat the air fryer to 200ºC. Line the air fryer basket with parchment paper. In a shallow bowl, whisk the cornmeal, Italian-style seasoning, paprika, salt, and pepper until blended. Place the beaten eggs in a second shallow bowl. Add the okra to the beaten egg and stir to coat. Add the egg and okra mixture to the cornmeal mixture and stir until coated. Place the okra on the parchment and spritz it with oil. Air fry for 4 minutes. Shake the basket, spritz the okra with oil, and air fry for 4 to 6 minutes more until lightly browned and crispy. Serve immediately.

## Scalloped Veggie Mix

**Prep time: 10 minutes | Cook time: 15 minutes | Serves 4**

1 Yukon Gold or other small white potato, thinly sliced
1 small sweet potato, peeled and thinly sliced
1 medium carrot, thinly sliced

60 ml minced onion
3 garlic cloves, minced
180 ml 2 percent milk
2 tablespoons cornflour
½ teaspoon dried thyme

Preheat the air fryer to 190ºC. In a baking pan, layer the potato, sweet potato, carrot, onion, and garlic. In a small bowl, whisk the milk, cornflour, and thyme until blended. Pour the milk mixture evenly over the vegetables in the pan. Bake for 15 minutes. Check the casserole—it should be golden brown on top, and the vegetables should be tender. Serve immediately.

## Buttery Sweet Potatoes

**Prep time: 5 minutes | Cook time: 10 minutes | Serves 4**

2 tablespoons butter, melted
1 tablespoon light brown sugar
2 sweet potatoes, peeled and cut
into ½-inch cubes
Cooking spray

Preheat the air fryer to 200°C. Line the air fryer basket with parchment paper. In a medium bowl, stir together the melted butter and brown sugar until blended. Toss the sweet potatoes in the butter mixture until coated. Place the sweet potatoes on the parchment and spritz with oil. Air fry for 5 minutes. Shake the basket, spritz the sweet potatoes with oil, and air fry for 5 minutes more until they're soft enough to cut with a fork. Serve immediately.

## Beef Bratwursts

**Prep time: 5 minutes | Cook time: 15 minutes | Serves 4**

4 (85 g) beef bratwursts

Preheat the air fryer to 190°C. Place the beef bratwursts in the air fryer basket and air fry for 15 minutes, turning once halfway through. Serve hot.

## Air Fried Courgette Sticks

**Prep time: 5 minutes | Cook time: 20 minutes | Serves 4**

1 medium courgette, cut into 48 sticks
60 ml seasoned breadcrumbs
1 tablespoon melted margarine
Cooking spray

Preheat the air fryer to 180°C. Spritz the air fryer basket with cooking spray and set aside. In 2 different shallow bowls, add the seasoned breadcrumbs and the margarine. One by one, dredge the courgette sticks into the margarine, then roll in the breadcrumbs to coat evenly. Arrange the crusted sticks on a plate. Place the courgette sticks in the prepared air fryer basket. Work in two batches to avoid overcrowding. Air fry for 10 minutes, or until golden brown and crispy. Shake the basket halfway through to cook evenly. When the cooking time is over, transfer the fries to a wire rack. Rest for 5 minutes and serve warm.

## Easy Roasted Asparagus

**Prep time: 5 minutes | Cook time: 6 minutes | Serves 4**

450 g asparagus, trimmed and halved crosswise
1 teaspoon extra-virgin olive oil
Salt and pepper, to taste
Lemon wedges, for serving

Preheat the air fryer to 200°C. Toss the asparagus with the oil, ⅛ teaspoon salt, and ⅛ teaspoon pepper in bowl. Transfer to air fryer basket. Place the basket in air fryer and roast for 6 to 8 minutes, or until tender and bright green, tossing halfway through cooking. Season with salt and pepper and serve with lemon wedges.

## Spinach and Carrot Balls

**Prep time: 10 minutes | Cook time: 10 minutes | Serves 4**

2 slices toasted bread
1 carrot, peeled and grated
1 package fresh spinach, blanched and chopped
½ onion, chopped
1 egg, beaten
½ teaspoon garlic powder
1 teaspoon minced garlic
1 teaspoon salt
½ teaspoon black pepper
1 tablespoon Engevita yeast flakes
1 tablespoon flour

Preheat the air fryer to 200°C. In a food processor, pulse the toasted bread to form breadcrumbs. Transfer into a shallow dish or bowl. In a bowl, mix together all the other ingredients. Use your hands to shape the mixture into small-sized balls. Roll the balls in the breadcrumbs, ensuring to cover them well. Put in the air fryer basket and air fry for 10 minutes. Serve immediately.

## Simple Pea Delight

**Prep time: 5 minutes | Cook time: 15 minutes |**

**Serves 2 to 4**

235 ml flour
1 teaspoon baking powder
3 eggs
235 ml coconut milk
235 ml soft white cheese
3 tablespoons pea protein
120 ml chicken or turkey strips
Pinch of sea salt
235 ml Mozzarella cheese

Preheat the air fryer to 200°C. In a large bowl, mix all ingredients together using a large wooden spoon. Spoon equal amounts of the mixture into muffin cups and bake for 15 minutes. Serve immediately.

## Air Fried Butternut Squash with Chopped Hazelnuts

**Prep time: 10 minutes | Cook time: 20 minutes |**

**Makes 700 ml**

2 tablespoons whole hazelnuts
700 ml butternut squash, peeled, deseeded, and cubed
¼ teaspoon rock salt
¼ teaspoon freshly ground black pepper
2 teaspoons olive oil
Cooking spray

Preheat the air fryer to 150°C. Spritz the air fryer basket with cooking spray. Arrange the hazelnuts in the preheated air fryer. Air fry for 3 minutes or until soft. Chopped the hazelnuts roughly and transfer to a small bowl. Set aside. Set the air fryer temperature to 180°C. Spritz with cooking spray. Put the butternut squash in a large bowl, then sprinkle with salt and pepper and drizzle with olive oil. Toss to coat well. Transfer the squash in the air fryer. Air fry for 20 minutes or until the squash is soft. Shake the basket halfway through the frying time. When the frying is complete, transfer the squash onto a plate and sprinkle with chopped hazelnuts before serving.

## Bacon Pinwheels

### Prep time: 10 minutes | Cook time: 10 minutes | Makes 8 pinwheels

1 sheet puff pastry
2 tablespoons maple syrup
60 ml brown sugar

8 slices bacon
Ground black pepper, to taste
Cooking spray

Preheat the air fryer to 180°C. Spritz the air fryer basket with cooking spray. Roll the puff pastry into a 10-inch square with a rolling pin on a clean work surface, then cut the pastry into 8 strips. Brush the strips with maple syrup and sprinkle with sugar, leaving a 1-inch far end uncovered. Arrange each slice of bacon on each strip, leaving a ⅛-inch length of bacon hang over the end close to you. Sprinkle with black pepper. From the end close to you, roll the strips into pinwheels, then dab the uncovered end with water and seal the rolls. Arrange the pinwheels in the preheated air fryer and spritz with cooking spray. Air fry for 10 minutes or until golden brown. Flip the pinwheels halfway through. Serve immediately.

## Baked Cheese Sandwich

### Prep time: 5 minutes | Cook time: 8 minutes | Serves 2

2 tablespoons mayonnaise
4 thick slices sourdough bread
4 thick slices Brie cheese

8 slices hot capicola or prosciutto

Preheat the air fryer to 175°C. Spread the mayonnaise on one side of each slice of bread. Place 2 slices of bread in the air fryer basket, mayonnaise-side down. Place the slices of Brie and capicola on the bread and cover with the remaining two slices of bread, mayonnaise-side up. Bake for 8 minutes, or until the cheese has melted. Serve immediately.

## Sweet Corn and Carrot Fritters

### Prep time: 10 minutes | Cook time: 8 to 11 minutes | Serves 4

### Prep time: 10 minutes | Cook time: 8 to 11 minutes | Serves 4

Preheat the air fryer to 175°C. Place the grated carrot in a colander and press down to squeeze out any excess moisture. Dry it with a paper towel. Combine the carrots with the remaining ingredients. Mould 1 tablespoon of the mixture into a ball and press it down with your hand or a spoon to flatten it. Repeat until the rest of the mixture is used up. Spritz the balls with cooking spray. Arrange in the air fryer basket, taking care not to overlap any balls. Bake for 8 to 11 minutes, or until they're firm. Serve warm.

## Easy Devils on Horseback

### Prep time: 5 minutes | Cook time: 7 minutes | Serves 12

24 small pitted prunes (128 g)
60 ml crumbled blue cheese, divided

8 slices centre-cut bacon, cut crosswise into thirds

Preheat the air fryer to 200°C. Halve the prunes lengthwise, but don't cut them all the way through. Place ½ teaspoon of cheese in the centre of each prune. Wrap a piece of bacon around each prune and secure the bacon with a toothpick. Working in batches, arrange a single layer of the prunes in the air fryer basket. Air fry for about 7 minutes, flipping halfway, until the bacon is cooked through and crisp. Let cool slightly and serve warm.

## Air Fried Broccoli

### Prep time: 5 minutes | Cook time: 6 minutes | Serves 1

4 egg yolks
60 ml butter, melted
475 ml coconut flour

Salt and pepper, to taste
475 ml broccoli florets

Preheat the air fryer to 200°C. In a bowl, whisk the egg yolks and melted butter together. Throw in the coconut flour, salt and pepper, then stir again to combine well. Dip each broccoli floret into the mixture and place in the air fryer basket. Air fry for 6 minutes in batches if necessary. Take care when removing them from the air fryer and serve immediately.

## Indian-Style Sweet Potato Fries

### Prep time: 5 minutes | Cook time: 8 minutes | Makes 20 fries

Seasoning Mixture:
¾ teaspoon ground coriander
½ teaspoon garam masala
½ teaspoon garlic powder
½ teaspoon ground cumin

¼ teaspoon ground cayenne pepper
Fries:
2 large sweet potatoes, peeled
2 teaspoons olive oil

Preheat the air fryer to 200°C. In a small bowl, combine the coriander, garam masala, garlic powder, cumin, and cayenne pepper. Slice the sweet potatoes into ¼-inch-thick fries. In a large bowl, toss the sliced sweet potatoes with the olive oil and the seasoning mixture. Transfer the seasoned sweet potatoes to the air fryer basket and fry for 8 minutes, until crispy. Serve warm.

# Chapter 7 Holiday Specials

## Golden Nuggets

**Prep time: 15 minutes | Cook time: 4 minutes per batch | Makes 20 nuggets**

235 ml plain flour, plus more for dusting
1 teaspoon baking powder
½ teaspoon butter, at room temperature, plus more for brushing

¼ teaspoon salt
60 ml water
⅛ teaspoon onion powder
¼ teaspoon garlic powder
⅛ teaspoon seasoning salt
Cooking spray

Preheat the air fryer to 190°C. Line the air fryer basket with parchment paper. Mix the flour, baking powder, butter, and salt in a large bowl. Stir to mix well. Gradually whisk in the water until a sanity dough forms. Put the dough on a lightly floured work surface, then roll it out into a ½-inch thick rectangle with a rolling pin. Cut the dough into about twenty 1- or 2-inch squares, then arrange the squares in a single layer in the preheated air fryer. Spritz with cooking spray. You need to work in batches to avoid overcrowding. Combine onion powder, garlic powder, and seasoning salt in a small bowl. Stir to mix well, then sprinkle the squares with the powder mixture. Air fry the dough squares for 4 minutes or until golden brown. Flip the squares halfway through the cooking time. Remove the golden nuggets from the air fryer and brush with more butter immediately. Serve warm.

## Teriyaki Shrimp Skewers

**Prep time: 10 minutes | Cook time: 6 minutes | Makes 12 skewered shrimp**

1½ tablespoons mirin
1½ teaspoons ginger paste
1½ tablespoons soy sauce
12 large shrimp, peeled and

deveined
1 large egg
180 ml panko breadcrumbs
Cooking spray

Combine the mirin, ginger paste, and soy sauce in a large bowl. Stir to mix well. Dunk the shrimp in the bowl of mirin mixture, then wrap the bowl in plastic and refrigerate for 1 hour to marinate. Preheat the air fryer to 200°C. Spritz the air fryer basket with cooking spray. Run twelve 4-inch skewers through each shrimp. Whisk the egg in the bowl of marinade to combine well. Pour the breadcrumbs on a plate. Dredge the shrimp skewers in the egg mixture, then shake the excess off and roll over the breadcrumbs to coat well. Arrange the shrimp skewers in the preheated air fryer and spritz with cooking spray. You need to work in batches to avoid overcrowding. Air fry for 6 minutes or until the shrimp are opaque and firm. Flip the shrimp skewers halfway through. Serve immediately.

## Kale Salad Sushi Rolls with Sriracha Mayonnaise

**Prep time: 10 minutes | Cook time: 10 minutes | Serves 12**

Kale Salad:
350 ml chopped kale
1 tablespoon sesame seeds
¾ teaspoon soy sauce
¾ teaspoon toasted sesame oil
½ teaspoon rice vinegar
¼ teaspoon ginger
⅛ teaspoon garlic powder
Sushi Rolls:

3 sheets sushi nori
1 batch cauliflower rice
½ avocado, sliced
Sriracha Mayonnaise:
60 ml Sriracha sauce
60 ml vegan mayonnaise
Coating:
120 ml panko breadcrumbs

Preheat the air fryer to 200°C. In a medium bowl, toss all the ingredients for the salad together until well coated and set aside. Place a sheet of nori on a clean work surface and spread the cauliflower rice in an even layer on the nori. Scoop 2 to 3 tablespoon of kale salad on the rice and spread over. Place 1 or 2 avocado slices on top. Roll up the sushi, pressing gently to get a nice, tight roll. Repeat to make the remaining 2 rolls. In a bowl, stir together the Sriracha sauce and mayonnaise until smooth. Add breadcrumbs to a separate bowl. Dredge the sushi rolls in Sriracha Mayonnaise, then roll in breadcrumbs till well coated. Place the coated sushi rolls in the air fryer basket and air fry for 10 minutes, or until golden brown and crispy. Flip the sushi rolls gently halfway through to ensure even cooking. Transfer to a platter and rest for 5 minutes before slicing each roll into 8 pieces. Serve warm.

## Classic Latkes

**Prep time: 15 minutes | Cook time: 10 minutes | Makes 4 latkes**

1 egg
2 tablespoons plain flour
2 medium potatoes, peeled and shredded, rinsed and drained

¼ teaspoon granulated garlic
½ teaspoon salt
Cooking spray

Preheat the air fryer to 190°C. Spritz the air fryer basket with cooking spray. Whisk together the egg, flour, potatoes, garlic, and salt in a large bowl. Stir to mix well. Divide the mixture into four parts, then flatten them into four circles. Arrange the circles into the preheated air fryer. Spritz the circles with cooking spray, then air fry for 10 minutes or until golden brown and crispy. Flip the latkes halfway through. Serve immediately.

## Garlicky Baked Cherry Tomatoes

**Prep time: 5 minutes | Cook time: 4 to 6 minutes |**
**Serves 2**

475 ml cherry tomatoes
1 clove garlic, thinly sliced
1 teaspoon olive oil
⅛ teaspoon rock salt

1 tablespoon freshly chopped
basil, for topping
Cooking spray

Preheat the air fryer to 180°C. Spritz the air fryer baking pan with cooking spray and set aside. In a large bowl, toss together the cherry tomatoes, sliced garlic, olive oil, and rock salt. Spread the mixture in an even layer in the prepared pan. Bake in the preheated air fryer for 4 to 6 minutes, or until the tomatoes become soft and wilted. Transfer to a bowl and rest for 5 minutes. Top with the chopped basil and serve warm.

## Mushroom and Green Bean Casserole

**Prep time: 10 minutes | Cook time: 15 minutes | Serves 4**

4 tablespoons unsalted butter
60 ml diced brown onion
120 ml chopped white
mushrooms
120 ml double cream
30 g full fat soft white cheese

120 ml chicken broth
¼ teaspoon xanthan gum
450 g fresh green beans, edges
trimmed
14 g pork crackling, finely
ground

In a medium skillet over medium heat, melt the butter. Sauté the onion and mushrooms until they become soft and fragrant, about 3 to 5 minutes. Add the double cream, soft white cheese, and broth to the pan. Whisk until smooth. Bring to a boil and then reduce to a simmer. Sprinkle the xanthan gum into the pan and remove from heat. Preheat the air fryer to 160°C. Chop the green beans into 2-inch pieces and place into a baking dish. Pour the sauce mixture over them and stir until coated. Top the dish with minced pork crackling. Put into the air fryer basket and bake for 15 minutes. Top will be golden and green beans fork-tender when fully cooked. Serve warm.

## Lush Snack Mix

**Prep time: 10 minutes | Cook time: 10 minutes |**
**Serves 10**

120 ml honey
3 tablespoons butter, melted
1 teaspoon salt
475 ml sesame sticks
475 ml pumpkin seeds

475 ml granola
235 ml cashews
475 ml crispy corn puff cereal
475 ml mini pretzel crisps

In a bowl, combine the honey, butter, and salt. In another bowl, mix the sesame sticks, pumpkin seeds, granola, cashews, corn puff cereal, and pretzel crisps. Combine the contents of the two bowls. Preheat the air fryer to 190°C. Put the mixture in the air fryer basket and air fry for 10 to 12 minutes to toast the snack mixture, shaking the basket frequently. Do this in two batches. Put the snack mix on a cookie sheet and allow it to cool fully. Serve immediately.

## Southwest Corn and Pepper Roast

**Prep time: 10 minutes | Cook time: 10 minutes | Serves 4**

For the Corn:
350 ml thawed frozen corn
kernels
235 ml mixed diced peppers
1 jalapeño, diced
235 ml diced brown onion
½ teaspoon ancho chilli powder
1 tablespoon fresh lemon juice

1 teaspoon ground cumin
½ teaspoon rock salt
Cooking spray
For Serving:
60 ml feta cheese
60 ml chopped fresh coriander
1 tablespoon fresh lemon juice

Preheat the air fryer to 190°C. Spritz the air fryer with cooking spray. Combine the ingredients for the corn in a large bowl. Stir to mix well. Pour the mixture into the air fryer. Air fry for 10 minutes or until the corn and peppers are soft. Shake the basket halfway through the cooking time. Transfer them onto a large plate, then spread with feta cheese and coriander. Drizzle with lemon juice and serve.

## Air Fried Blistered Tomatoes

**Prep time: 5 minutes | Cook time: 10 minutes |**
**Serves 4 to 6**

900 g cherry tomatoes
2 tablespoons olive oil
2 teaspoons balsamic vinegar

½ teaspoon salt
½ teaspoon ground black
pepper

Preheat the air fryer with a cake pan to 200°C. Toss the cherry tomatoes with olive oil in a large bowl to coat well. Pour the tomatoes in the cake pan. Air fry the cherry tomatoes for 10 minutes or until the tomatoes are blistered and lightly wilted. Shake the basket halfway through. Transfer the blistered tomatoes to a large bowl and toss with balsamic vinegar, salt, and black pepper before serving.

## Hasselback Potatoes

**Prep time: 5 minutes | Cook time: 50 minutes | Serves 4**

4 russet or Maris Piper potatoes,
peeled
Salt and freshly ground black

pepper, to taste
60 ml grated Parmesan cheese
Cooking spray

Preheat the air fryer to 200°C. Spray the air fryer basket lightly with cooking spray. Make thin parallel cuts into each potato, ⅛-inch to ¼-inch apart, stopping at about ½ of the way through. The potato needs to stay intact along the bottom. Spray the potatoes with cooking spray and use the hands or a silicone brush to completely coat the potatoes lightly in oil. Put the potatoes, sliced side up, in the air fryer basket in a single layer. Leave a little room between each potato. Sprinkle the potatoes lightly with salt and black pepper. Air fry for 20 minutes. Reposition the potatoes and spritz lightly with cooking spray again. Air fry until the potatoes are fork-tender and crispy and browned, another 20 to 30 minutes. Sprinkle the potatoes with Parmesan cheese and serve.

## Jewish Blintzes

**Prep time: 5 minutes | Cook time: 10 minutes |**
**Makes 8 blintzes**

2 (213 g) packages farmer or ricotta cheese, mashed
60 ml soft white cheese
¼ teaspoon vanilla extract

60 ml granulated white sugar
8 egg roll wrappers
4 tablespoons butter, melted

Preheat the air fryer to 190ºC. Combine the cheese, soft white cheese, vanilla extract, and sugar in a bowl. Stir to mix well. Unfold the egg roll wrappers on a clean work surface, spread 60 ml filling at the edge of each wrapper and leave a ½-inch edge uncovering. Wet the edges of the wrappers with water and fold the uncovered edge over the filling. Fold the left and right sides in the centre, then tuck the edge under the filling and fold to wrap the filling. Brush the wrappers with melted butter, then arrange the wrappers in a single layer in the preheated air fryer, seam side down. Leave a little space between each two wrappers. Work in batches to avoid overcrowding. Air fry for 10 minutes or until golden brown. Serve immediately.

## Easy Cinnamon Toast

**Prep time: 5 minutes | Cook time: 20 minutes | Serves 6**

1½ teaspoons cinnamon
1½ teaspoons vanilla extract
120 ml sugar
2 teaspoons ground black

pepper
2 tablespoons melted coconut oil
12 slices wholemeal bread

Preheat the air fryer to 200ºC. Combine all the ingredients, except for the bread, in a large bowl. Stir to mix well. Dunk the bread in the bowl of mixture gently to coat and infuse well. Shake the excess off. Arrange the bread slices in the preheated air fryer. Air fry for 5 minutes or until golden brown. Flip the bread halfway through. You may need to cook in batches to avoid overcrowding. Remove the bread slices from the air fryer and slice to serve.

## Whole Chicken Roast

**Prep time: 10 minutes | Cook time: 1 hour | Serves 6**

1 teaspoon salt
1 teaspoon Italian seasoning
½ teaspoon freshly ground black pepper
½ teaspoon paprika

½ teaspoon garlic powder
½ teaspoon onion powder
2 tablespoons olive oil, plus more as needed
1 (1.8 kg) small chicken

Preheat the air fryer to 180ºC. Grease the air fryer basket lightly with olive oil. In a small bowl, mix the salt, Italian seasoning, pepper, paprika, garlic powder, and onion powder. Remove any giblets from the chicken. Pat the chicken dry thoroughly with paper towels, including the cavity. Brush the chicken all over with the olive oil and rub it with the seasoning mixture. Truss the chicken or tie the legs with butcher's twine. This will make it easier to flip the chicken during cooking. Put the chicken in the air fryer basket, breast-side down. Air fry for 30 minutes. Flip the chicken over and baste it with any drippings collected in the bottom drawer of the air fryer. Lightly brush the chicken with olive oil. Air fry for 20 minutes. Flip the chicken over one last time and air fry until a thermometer inserted into the thickest part of the thigh reaches at least 75ºC and it's crispy and golden, 10 more minutes. Continue to cook, checking every 5 minutes until the chicken reaches the correct internal temperature. Let the chicken rest for 10 minutes before carving and serving.

## Supplì al Telefono (Risotto Croquettes)

**Prep time: 1 hour 40 minutes | Cook time: 1 hour |**
**Serves 6**

Risotto Croquettes:
4 tablespoons unsalted butter
1 small brown onion, minced
235 ml Arborio rice
820 ml chicken stock
120 ml dry white wine
3 eggs
Zest of 1 lemon
120 ml grated Parmesan cheese
60 g fresh Mozzarella cheese
60 ml peas
2 tablespoons water
120 ml plain flour
350 ml panko breadcrumbs

Rock salt and ground black pepper, to taste
Cooking spray
Tomato Sauce:
2 tablespoons extra-virgin olive oil
4 cloves garlic, minced
¼ teaspoon red pepper flakes
1 (794 g) can crushed tomatoes or passata
2 teaspoons granulated sugar
Rock salt and ground black pepper, to taste

Melt the butter in a pot over medium heat, then add the onion and salt to taste. Sauté for 5 minutes or until the onion is translucent. Add the rice and stir to coat well. Cook for 3 minutes or until the rice is lightly browned. Pour in the chicken stock and wine. Bring to a boil. Then cook for 20 minutes or until the rice is tender and liquid is almost absorbed. Make the risotto: When the rice is cooked, break the egg into the pot. Add the lemon zest and Parmesan cheese. Sprinkle with salt and ground black pepper. Stir to mix well. Pour the risotto in a baking sheet, then level with a spatula to spread the risotto evenly. Wrap the baking sheet in plastic and refrigerate for1 hour. Meanwhile, heat the olive oil in a saucepan over medium heat until shimmering. Add the garlic and sprinkle with red pepper flakes. Sauté for a minute or until fragrant. Add the crushed tomatoes and sprinkle with sugar. Stir to mix well. Bring to a boil. Reduce the heat to low and simmer for 15 minutes or until lightly thickened. Sprinkle with salt and pepper to taste. Set aside until ready to serve. Remove the risotto from the refrigerator. Scoop the risotto into twelve 2-inch balls, then flatten the balls with your hands. Arrange a about ½-inch piece of Mozzarella and 5 peas in the centre of each flattened ball, then wrap them back into balls. Transfer the balls in a baking sheet lined with parchment paper, then refrigerate for 15 minutes or until firm. Preheat the air fryer to 200ºC. Whisk the remaining 2 eggs with 2 tablespoons of water in a bowl. Pour the flour in a second bowl and pour the panko in a third bowl. Dredge the risotto balls in the bowl of flour first, then into the eggs, and then into the panko. Shake the excess off. Transfer the balls in the preheated air fryer and spritz with cooking spray. You may need to work in batches to avoid overcrowding. Bake for 10 minutes or until golden brown. Flip the balls halfway through. Serve the risotto balls with the tomato sauce.

## Eggnog Bread

**Prep time: 10 minutes | Cook time: 18 minutes |**

**Serves 6 to 8**

| | |
|---|---|
| 235 ml flour, plus more for dusting | 1 tablespoon plus 1 teaspoon butter, melted |
| 60 ml sugar | 60 ml pecans |
| 1 teaspoon baking powder | 60 ml chopped candied fruit (cherries, pineapple, or mixed fruits) |
| ¼ teaspoon salt | |
| ¼ teaspoon nutmeg | |
| 120 ml eggnog | Cooking spray |
| 1 egg yolk | |

Preheat the air fryer to 180ºC. In a medium bowl, stir together the flour, sugar, baking powder, salt, and nutmeg. Add eggnog, egg yolk, and butter. Mix well but do not beat. Stir in nuts and fruit. Spray a baking pan with cooking spray and dust with flour. Spread batter into prepared pan and bake for 18 minutes or until top is dark golden brown and bread starts to pull away from sides of pan. Serve immediately.

## Air Fried Spicy Olives

**Prep time: 10 minutes | Cook time: 5 minutes | Serves 4**

| | |
|---|---|
| 340 g pitted black extra-large olives | 1 teaspoon red pepper flakes |
| 60 ml plain flour | 1 teaspoon smoked paprika |
| 235 ml panko breadcrumbs | 1 egg beaten with 1 tablespoon water |
| 2 teaspoons dried thyme | Vegetable oil for spraying |

Preheat the air fryer to 200ºC. Drain the olives and place them on a paper towel–lined plate to dry. Put the flour on a plate. Combine the panko, thyme, red pepper flakes, and paprika on a separate plate. Dip an olive in the flour, shaking off any excess, then coat with egg mixture. Dredge the olive in the panko mixture, pressing to make the crumbs adhere, and place the breaded olive on a platter. Repeat with the remaining olives. Spray the olives with oil and place them in a single layer in the air fryer basket. Work in batches if necessary so as not to overcrowd the basket. Air fry for 5 minutes until the breading is browned and crispy. Serve warm

## Simple Air Fried Crispy Brussels Sprouts

**Prep time: 5 minutes | Cook time: 20 minutes | Serves 4**

| | |
|---|---|
| ¼ teaspoon salt | oil |
| ⅛ teaspoon ground black pepper | 450 g Brussels sprouts, trimmed and halved |
| 1 tablespoon extra-virgin olive | Lemon wedges, for garnish |

Preheat the air fryer to 175ºC. Combine the salt, black pepper, and olive oil in a large bowl. Stir to mix well. Add the Brussels sprouts to the bowl of mixture and toss to coat well. Arrange the Brussels sprouts in the preheated air fryer. Air fry for 20 minutes or until lightly browned and wilted. Shake the basket two times during the air frying. Transfer the cooked Brussels sprouts to a large plate and squeeze the lemon wedges on top to serve.

## Golden Salmon and Carrot Croquettes

**Prep time: 15 minutes | Cook time: 10 minutes | Serves 6**

| | |
|---|---|
| 2 egg whites | 2 tablespoons minced garlic cloves |
| 235 ml almond flour | |
| 235 ml panko breadcrumbs | 120 ml chopped onion |
| 450 g chopped salmon fillet | 2 tablespoons chopped chives |
| 160 ml grated carrots | Cooking spray |

Preheat the air fryer to 175ºC. Spritz the air fryer basket with cooking spray. Whisk the egg whites in a bowl. Put the flour in a second bowl. Pour the breadcrumbs in a third bowl. Set aside. Combine the salmon, carrots, garlic, onion, and chives in a large bowl. Stir to mix well. Form the mixture into balls with your hands. Dredge the balls into the flour, then egg, and then breadcrumbs to coat well. Arrange the salmon balls in the preheated air fryer and spritz with cooking spray. Air fry for 10 minutes or until crispy and browned. Shake the basket halfway through. Serve immediately.

## Custard Donut Holes with Chocolate Glaze

**Prep time: 1 hour 50 minutes | Cook time: 4 minutes**

**per batch | Makes 24 donut holes**

| Dough: | Custard Filling: |
|---|---|
| 350 ml bread flour | 1 (96 g) box French vanilla |
| 2 egg yolks | instant pudding mix |
| 1 teaspoon active dry yeast | 60 ml double cream |
| 120 ml warm milk | 180 ml whole milk |
| ½ teaspoon pure vanilla extract | Chocolate Glaze: |
| 2 tablespoons butter, melted | 80 ml double cream |
| 1 tablespoon sugar | 235 ml chocolate chips |
| ¼ teaspoon salt | Special Equipment: |
| Cooking spray | A pastry bag with a long tip |

Combine the ingredients for the dough in a food processor, then pulse until a satiny dough ball forms. Transfer the dough on a lightly floured work surface, then knead for 2 minutes by hand and shape the dough back to a ball. Spritz a large bowl with cooking spray, then transfer the dough ball into the bowl. Wrap the bowl in plastic and let it rise for 1½ hours or until it doubled in size. Transfer the risen dough on a floured work surface, then shape it into a 24-inch-long log. Cut the log into 24 parts and shape each part into a ball. Transfer the balls on two or three baking sheets and let sit to rise for 30 more minutes. Preheat the air fryer to 200ºC. Arrange the baking sheets in the air fryer. You need to work in batches to avoid overcrowding. Spritz the balls with cooking spray. Bake for 4 minutes or until golden brown. Flip the balls halfway through. Meanwhile, combine the ingredients for the filling in a large bowl and whisk for 2 minutes with a hand mixer until well combined. Pour the double cream in a saucepan, then bring to a boil. Put the chocolate chips in a small bowl and pour in the boiled double cream immediately. Mix until the chocolate chips are melted, and the mixture is smooth. Transfer the baked donut holes to a large plate, then pierce a hole into each donut hole and lightly hollow them. Pour the filling in a pastry bag with a long tip and gently squeeze the filling into the donut holes. Then top the donut holes with chocolate glaze. Allow to sit for 10 minutes, then serve.

## South Carolina Shrimp and Corn Bake

**Prep time: 10 minutes | Cook time: 18 minutes | Serves 2**

1 ear corn, husk and silk removed, cut into 2-inch rounds
227 g red potatoes, unpeeled, cut into 1-inch pieces
2 teaspoons Old Bay or all-purpose seasoning, divided
2 teaspoons vegetable oil, divided
¼ teaspoon ground black

pepper
227 g large shrimps (about 12 shrimps), deveined
170 g andouille or chorizo sausage, cut into 1-inch pieces
2 garlic cloves, minced
1 tablespoon chopped fresh parsley

Preheat the air fryer to 200ºC. Put the corn rounds and potatoes in a large bowl. Sprinkle with 1 teaspoon of seasoning and drizzle with vegetable oil. Toss to coat well. Transfer the corn rounds and potatoes on a baking sheet, then put in the preheated air fryer. Bake for 12 minutes or until soft and browned. Shake the basket halfway through the cooking time. Meanwhile, cut slits into the shrimps but be careful not to cut them through. Combine the shrimps, sausage, remaining seasoning, and remaining vegetable oil in the large bowl. Toss to coat well. When the baking of the potatoes and corn rounds is complete, add the shrimps and sausage and bake for 6 more minutes or until the shrimps are opaque. Shake the basket halfway through the cooking time. When the baking is finished, serve them on a plate and spread with parsley before serving.

## Frico

**Prep time: 5 minutes | Cook time: 5 minutes | Serves 2**

235 ml shredded aged Manchego cheese
1 teaspoon plain flour

½ teaspoon cumin seeds
¼ teaspoon cracked black pepper

Preheat the air fryer to 190ºC. Line the air fryer basket with parchment paper. Combine the cheese and flour in a bowl. Stir to mix well. Spread the mixture in the basket into a 4-inch round. Combine the cumin and black pepper in a small bowl. Stir to mix well. Sprinkle the cumin mixture over the cheese round. Air fry 5 minutes or until the cheese is lightly browned and frothy. Use tongs to transfer the cheese wafer onto a plate and slice to serve.

## Crispy Green Tomato Slices

**Prep time: 10 minutes | Cook time: 8 minutes |**
**Makes 12 slices**

120 ml plain flour
1 egg
120 ml buttermilk
235 ml cornmeal
235 ml panko breadcrumbs
2 green tomatoes, cut into

¼-inch-thick slices, patted dry
½ teaspoon salt
½ teaspoon ground black pepper
Cooking spray

Preheat the air fryer to 200ºC. Line the air fryer basket with parchment paper. Pour the flour in a bowl. Whisk the egg and buttermilk in a second bowl. Combine the cornmeal and panko breadcrumbs in a third bowl. Dredge the tomato slices in the bowl of flour first, then into the egg mixture, and then dunk the slices into the cornmeal mixture. Shake the excess off. Transfer the well-coated tomato slices in the preheated air fryer and sprinkle with salt and ground black pepper. Spritz the tomato slices with cooking spray. Air fry for 8 minutes or until crispy and lightly browned. Flip the slices halfway through the cooking time. Serve immediately.

## Simple Butter Cake

**Prep time: 25 minutes | Cook time: 20 minutes | Serves 8**

235 ml plain flour
1¼ teaspoons baking powder
¼ teaspoon salt
120 ml plus 1½ tablespoons granulated white sugar
9½ tablespoons butter, at room

temperature
2 large eggs
1 large egg yolk
2½ tablespoons milk
1 teaspoon vanilla extract
Cooking spray

Preheat the air fryer to 165ºC. Spritz a cake pan with cooking spray. Combine the flour, baking powder, and salt in a large bowl. Stir to mix well. Whip the sugar and butter in a separate bowl with a hand mixer on medium speed for 3 minutes. Whip the eggs, egg yolk, milk, and vanilla extract into the sugar and butter mix with a hand mixer. Pour in the flour mixture and whip with hand mixer until sanity and smooth. Scrape the batter into the cake pan and level the batter with a spatula. Place the cake pan in the preheated air fryer. Bake for 20 minutes or until a toothpick inserted in the centre comes out clean. Check the doneness during the last 5 minutes of the baking. Invert the cake on a cooling rack and allow to cool for 15 minutes before slicing to serve.

## Arancini

**Prep time: 5 minutes | Cook time: 30 minutes |**
**Makes 10 arancini**

160 ml raw white Arborio rice
2 teaspoons butter
½ teaspoon salt
315 ml water
2 large eggs, well beaten
300 ml dried breadcrumbs

mixed with Italian-style seasoning
10 ¾-inch semi-firm Mozzarella cubes
Cooking spray

Pour the rice, butter, salt, and water in a pot. Stir to mix well and bring a boil over medium-high heat. Keep stirring. Reduce the heat to low and cover the pot. Simmer for 20 minutes or until the rice is tender. Turn off the heat and let sit, covered, for 10 minutes, then open the lid and fluffy the rice with a fork. Allow to cool for 10 more minutes. Preheat the air fryer to 190ºC. Pour the beaten eggs in a bowl, then pour the breadcrumbs in a separate bowl. Scoop 2 tablespoons of the cooked rice up and form it into a ball, then press the Mozzarella into the ball and wrap. Dredge the ball in the eggs first, then shake the excess off the dunk the ball in the breadcrumbs. Roll to coat evenly. Repeat to make 10 balls in total with remaining rice. Transfer the balls in the preheated air fryer and spritz with cooking spray. You need to work in batches to avoid overcrowding. Air fry for 10 minutes or until the balls are lightly browned and crispy. Remove the balls from the air fryer and allow to cool before serving.

# Parsnip Fries with Garlic-Yoghurt Dip

### Prep timeParsnip Fries with Garlic-Yoghurt Dip

| | |
|---|---|
| 3 medium parsnips, peeled, cut into sticks | 60 ml plain Greek yoghurt |
| ¼ teaspoon rock salt | ⅛ teaspoon garlic powder |
| 1 teaspoon olive oil | 1 tablespoon sour cream |
| 1 garlic clove, unpeeled | ¼ teaspoon rock salt |
| Cooking spray | Freshly ground black pepper, to taste |
| Dip: | |

Preheat the air fryer to 180°C. Spritz the air fryer basket with cooking spray. Put the parsnip sticks in a large bowl, then sprinkle with salt and drizzle with olive oil. Transfer the parsnip into the preheated air fryer and add the garlic. Air fry for 5 minutes, then remove the garlic from the air fryer and shake the basket. Air fry for 5 more minutes or until the parsnip sticks are crisp. Meanwhile, peel the garlic and crush it. Combine the crushed garlic with the ingredients for the dip. Stir to mix well. When the frying is complete, remove the parsnip fries from the air fryer and serve with the dipping sauce.

# Lemony and Garlicky Asparagus

### Prep time: 5 minutes | Cook time: 10 minutes | Makes 10 spears

| | |
|---|---|
| 10 spears asparagus (about 230 g in total), snap the ends off | ½ teaspoon salt |
| 1 tablespoon lemon juice | ¼ teaspoon ground black pepper |
| 2 teaspoons minced garlic | Cooking spray |

Preheat the air fryer to 200°C. Line a parchment paper in the air fryer basket. Put the asparagus spears in a large bowl. Drizzle with lemon juice and sprinkle with minced garlic, salt, and ground black pepper. Toss to coat well. Transfer the asparagus in the preheated air fryer and spritz with cooking spray. Air fryer for 10 minutes or until wilted and soft. Flip the asparagus halfway through. Serve immediately.

# Hearty Honey Yeast Rolls

### Prep time: 10 minutes | Cook time: 20 minutes | Makes 8 rolls

| | |
|---|---|
| 60 ml whole milk, heated to 45°C in the microwave | ½ teaspoon rock salt |
| ½ teaspoon active dry yeast | 2 tablespoons unsalted butter, at room temperature, plus more for greasing |
| 1 tablespoon honey | |
| 160 ml plain flour, plus more for dusting | Flaky sea salt, to taste |

In a large bowl, whisk together the milk, yeast, and honey and let stand until foamy, about 10 minutes. Stir in the flour and salt until just combined. Stir in the butter until absorbed. Scrape the dough onto a lightly floured work surface and knead until smooth, about 6 minutes. Transfer the dough to a lightly greased bowl, cover loosely with a sheet of plastic wrap or a kitchen towel, and let sit until nearly doubled in size, about 1 hour. Uncover the dough, lightly press it down to expel the bubbles, then portion it into 8 equal pieces. Prep the work surface by wiping it clean with a damp paper towel (if there is flour on the work surface, it will prevent the dough from sticking lightly to the surface, which helps it form a ball). Roll each piece into a ball by cupping the palm of the hand around the dough against the work surface and moving the heel of the hand in a circular motion while using the thumb to contain the dough and tighten it into a perfectly round ball. Once all the balls are formed, nestle them side by side in the air fryer basket. Cover the rolls loosely with a kitchen towel or a sheet of plastic wrap and let sit until lightly risen and puffed, 20 to 30 minutes. Preheat the air fryer to 130°C. Uncover the rolls and gently brush with more butter, being careful not to press the rolls too hard. Air fry until the rolls are light golden brown and fluffy, about 12 minutes. Remove the rolls from the air fryer and brush liberally with more butter, if you like, and sprinkle each roll with a pinch of sea salt. Serve warm.

# Garlicky Zoodles

### Prep time: 10 minutes | Cook time: 10 minutes | Serves 4

| | |
|---|---|
| 2 large courgette, peeled and spiralized | ½ teaspoon rock salt |
| | 1 garlic clove, whole |
| 2 large yellow butternut squash, peeled and spiralized | 2 tablespoons fresh basil, chopped |
| 1 tablespoon olive oil, divided | Cooking spray |

Preheat the air fryer to 180°C. Spritz the air fryer basket with cooking spray. Combine the courgette and butternut squash with 1 teaspoon olive oil and salt in a large bowl. Toss to coat well. Transfer the courgette and butternut squash in the preheated air fryer and add the garlic. Air fry for 10 minutes or until tender and fragrant. Toss the spiralized courgette and butternut squash halfway through the cooking time. Transfer the cooked courgette and butternut squash onto a plate and set aside. Remove the garlic from the air fryer and allow to cool for a few minutes. Mince the garlic and combine with remaining olive oil in a small bowl. Stir to mix well. Drizzle the spiralized courgette and butternut squash with garlic oil and sprinkle with basil. Toss to serve.

# Easy Air Fried Edamame

### Prep time: 5 minutes | Cook time: 7 minutes | Serves 6

| | |
|---|---|
| 680 g unshelled edamame | 1 teaspoon sea salt |
| 2 tablespoons olive oil | |

Preheat the air fryer to 200°C. Place the edamame in a large bowl, then drizzle with olive oil. Toss to coat well. Transfer the edamame to the preheated air fryer. Cook for 7 minutes or until tender and warmed through. Shake the basket at least three times during the cooking. Transfer the cooked edamame onto a plate and sprinkle with salt. Toss to combine well and set aside for 3 minutes to infuse before serving.

# Cinnamon Rolls with Cream Glaze

**Prep time: 2 hours 15 minutes | Cook time: 10 minutes | Serves 8**

450 g frozen bread dough, thawed
2 tablespoons melted butter
1½ tablespoons cinnamon
180 ml brown sugar
Cooking spray

Cream Glaze:
110 g soft white cheese
½ teaspoon vanilla extract
2 tablespoons melted butter
300 ml powdered erythritol

Place the bread dough on a clean work surface, then roll the dough out into a rectangle with a rolling pin. Brush the top of the dough with melted butter and leave 1-inch edges uncovered. Combine the cinnamon and sugar in a small bowl, then sprinkle the dough with the cinnamon mixture. Roll the dough over tightly, then cut the dough log into 8 portions. Wrap the portions in plastic, better separately, and let sit to rise for 1 or 2 hours. Meanwhile, combine the ingredients for the glaze in a separate small bowl. Stir to mix well. Preheat the air fryer to 175ºC. Spritz the air fryer basket with cooking spray. Transfer the risen rolls to the preheated air fryer. You may need to work in batches to avoid overcrowding. Air fry for 5 minutes or until golden brown. Flip the rolls halfway through. Serve the rolls with the glaze.

# Chapter 8 Desserts

## Chocolate and Rum Cupcakes

**Prep time: 5 minutes | Cook time: 15 minutes | Serves 6**

| | |
|---|---|
| 150 g granulated sweetener | ⅛ teaspoon salt |
| 140 g almond flour | 120 ml milk |
| 1 teaspoon unsweetened baking powder | 110 g butter, at room temperature |
| 3 teaspoons cocoa powder | 3 eggs, whisked |
| ½ teaspoon baking soda | 1 teaspoon pure rum extract |
| ½ teaspoon ground cinnamon | 70 g blueberries |
| ¼ teaspoon grated nutmeg | Cooking spray |

Preheat the air fryer to 175°C. Spray a 6-cup muffin tin with cooking spray. In a mixing bowl, combine the sweetener, almond flour, baking powder, cocoa powder, baking soda, cinnamon, nutmeg, and salt and stir until well blended. In another mixing bowl, mix together the milk, butter, egg, and rum extract until thoroughly combined. Slowly and carefully pour this mixture into the bowl of dry mixture. Stir in the blueberries. Spoon the batter into the greased muffin cups, filling each about three-quarters full. Bake for 15 minutes, or until the center is springy and a toothpick inserted in the middle comes out clean. Remove from the basket and place on a wire rack to cool. Serve immediately.

## Simple Pineapple Sticks

**Prep time: 5 minutes | Cook time: 10 minutes | Serves 4**

| | |
|---|---|
| ½ fresh pineapple, cut into sticks | 25 g desiccated coconut |

Preheat the air fryer to 200°C. Coat the pineapple sticks in the desiccated coconut and put each one in the air fryer basket. Air fry for 10 minutes. Serve immediately

## Pumpkin-Spice Bread Pudding

**Prep time: 15 minutes | Cook time: 35 minutes | Serves 6**

| | |
|---|---|
| Bread Pudding: | 1/3 loaf of day-old baguette or crusty country bread, cubed |
| 175 ml heavy whipping cream | |
| 120 g canned pumpkin | 4 tablespoons unsalted butter, melted |
| 80 ml whole milk | |
| 65 g granulated sugar | Sauce: |
| 1 large egg plus 1 yolk | 80 ml pure maple syrup |
| ½ teaspoon pumpkin pie spice | 1 tablespoon unsalted butter |
| ⅛ teaspoon kosher, or coarse sea salt | 120 ml heavy whipping cream |
| | ½ teaspoon pure vanilla extract |

For the bread pudding: In a medium bowl, combine the cream, pumpkin, milk, sugar, egg and yolk, pumpkin pie spice, and salt. Whisk until well combined. In a large bowl, toss the bread cubes with the melted butter. Add the pumpkin mixture and gently toss until the ingredients are well combined. Transfer the mixture to a baking pan. Place the pan in the air fryer basket. Set the fryer to 175°C cooking for 35 minutes, or until custard is set in the middle. Meanwhile, for the sauce: In a small saucepan, combine the syrup and butter. Heat over medium heat, stirring, until the butter melts. Stir in the cream and simmer, stirring often, until the sauce has thickened, about 15 minutes. Stir in the vanilla. Remove the pudding from the air fryer. Let the pudding stand for 10 minutes before serving with the warm sauce.

## Crispy Pineapple Rings

**Prep time: 5 minutes | Cook time: 6 to 8 minutes | Serves 6**

| | |
|---|---|
| 240 ml rice milk | ½ teaspoon vanilla essence |
| 85 g plain flour | ½ teaspoon ground cinnamon |
| 120 ml water | ¼ teaspoon ground star anise |
| 25 g unsweetened flaked coconut | Pinch of kosher, or coarse sea salt |
| 4 tablespoons granulated sugar | 1 medium pineapple, peeled and sliced |
| ½ teaspoon baking soda | |
| ½ teaspoon baking powder | |

Preheat the air fryer to 190°C. In a large bowl, stir together all the ingredients except the pineapple. Dip each pineapple slice into the batter until evenly coated. Arrange the pineapple slices in the basket and air fry for 6 to 8 minutes until golden brown. Remove from the basket to a plate and cool for 5 minutes before serving warm

## Baked Brazilian Pineapple

**Prep time: 10 minutes | Cook time: 10 minutes | Serves 4**

| | |
|---|---|
| 95 g brown sugar | cored, and cut into spears |
| 2 teaspoons ground cinnamon | 3 tablespoons unsalted butter, melted |
| 1 small pineapple, peeled, | |

In a small bowl, mix the brown sugar and cinnamon until thoroughly combined. Brush the pineapple spears with the melted butter. Sprinkle the cinnamon-sugar over the spears, pressing lightly to ensure it adheres well. Place the spears in the air fryer basket in a single layer. (Depending on the size of your air fryer, you may have to do this in batches.) Set the air fryer to 200°C and cook for 10 minutes for the first batch (6 to 8 minutes for the next batch, as the fryer will be preheated). Halfway through the cooking time, brush the spears with butter. The pineapple spears are done when they are heated through, and the sugar is bubbling. Serve hot.

## Mini Peanut Butter Tarts

**Prep time: 25 minutes | Cook time: 12 to 15 minutes | Serves 8**

| | |
|---|---|
| 125 g pecans | cheese |
| 110 g finely ground blanched | 110 g cream cheese |
| almond flour | 140 g sugar-free peanut butter |
| 2 tablespoons unsalted butter, at | 1 teaspoon pure vanilla extract |
| room temperature | ⅛ teaspoon sea salt |
| 50 g powdered sweetener, plus | 85 g organic chocolate chips |
| 2 tablespoons, divided | 1 tablespoon coconut oil |
| 120 g heavy (whipping) cream | 40 g chopped peanuts or pecans |
| 2 tablespoons mascarpone | |

Place the pecans in the bowl of a food processor; process until they are finely ground. Transfer the ground pecans to a medium bowl and stir in the almond flour. Add the butter and 2 tablespoons of sweetener and stir until the mixture becomes wet and crumbly. Divide the mixture among 8 silicone muffin cups, pressing the crust firmly with your fingers into the bottom and part way up the sides of each cup. Arrange the muffin cups in the air fryer basket, working in batches if necessary. Set the air fryer to 150°C and bake for 12 to 15 minutes, until the crusts begin to brown. Remove the cups from the air fryer and set them aside to cool. In the bowl of a stand mixer, combine the heavy cream and mascarpone cheese. Beat until peaks form. Transfer to a large bowl. In the same stand mixer bowl, combine the cream cheese, peanut butter, remaining 50 g sweetener, vanilla, and salt. Beat at medium-high speed until smooth. Reduce the speed to low and add the heavy cream mixture back a spoonful at a time, beating after each addition. Spoon the peanut butter mixture over the crusts and freeze the tarts for 30 minutes. Place the chocolate chips and coconut oil in the top of a double boiler over high heat. Stir until melted, then remove from the heat. 1Drizzle the melted chocolate over the peanut butter tarts. Top with the chopped nuts and freeze the tarts for another 15 minutes, until set. 1Store the peanut butter tarts in an airtight container in the refrigerator for up to 1 week or in the freezer for up to 1 month.

## Glazed Cherry Turnovers

**Prep time: 10 minutes | Cook time: 14 minutes per batch | Serves 8**

| | |
|---|---|
| 2 sheets frozen puff pastry, | 1 egg, beaten |
| thawed | 90 g sliced almonds |
| 600 g can premium cherry pie | 120 g icing sugar |
| filling | 2 tablespoons milk |
| 2 teaspoons ground cinnamon | |

Roll a sheet of puff pastry out into a square that is approximately 10-inches by 10-inches. Cut this large square into quarters. Mix the cherry pie filling and cinnamon together in a bowl. Spoon ¼ cup of the cherry filling into the center of each puff pastry square. Brush the perimeter of the pastry square with the egg wash. Fold one corner of the puff pastry over the cherry pie filling towards the opposite corner, forming a triangle. Seal the two edges of the pastry together with the tip of a fork, making a design with the tines. Brush the top of the turnovers with the egg wash and sprinkle sliced almonds over each one. Repeat these steps with the second sheet of puff pastry. You should have eight turnovers at the end. Preheat the air fryer to 190°C. Air fry two turnovers at a time for 14 minutes, carefully turning them over halfway through the cooking time. While the turnovers are cooking, make the glaze by whisking the icing sugar and milk together in a small bowl until smooth. Let the glaze sit for a minute so the sugar can absorb the milk. If the consistency is still too thick to drizzle, add a little more milk, a drop at a time, and stir until smooth. Let the cooked cherry turnovers sit for at least 10 minutes. Then drizzle the glaze over each turnover in a zigzag motion. Serve warm or at room temperature.

## Berry Crumble

**Prep time: 10 minutes | Cook time: 15 minutes | Serves 4**

| | |
|---|---|
| For the Filling: | 20 g rolled oats |
| 300 g mixed berries | 1 tablespoon granulated sugar |
| 2 tablespoons sugar | 2 tablespoons cold unsalted |
| 1 tablespoon cornflour | butter, cut into small cubes |
| 1 tablespoon fresh lemon juice | Whipped cream or ice cream |
| For the Topping | (optional) |
| 30 g plain flour | |

Preheat the air fryer to 200°C. For the filling: In a round baking pan, gently mix the berries, sugar, cornflour, and lemon juice until thoroughly combined. For the topping: In a small bowl, combine the flour, oats, and sugar. Stir the butter into the flour mixture until the mixture has the consistency of breadcrumbs. Sprinkle the topping over the berries. Put the pan in the air fryer basket and air fry for 15 minutes. Let cool for 5 minutes on a wire rack. Serve topped with whipped cream or ice cream, if desired.

## Roasted Honey Pears

**Prep time: 7 minutes | Cook time: 18 to 23 minutes | Serves 4**

| | |
|---|---|
| 2 large Bosc pears, halved | ½ teaspoon ground cinnamon |
| lengthwise and seeded | 30 g walnuts, chopped |
| 3 tablespoons honey | 55 g part-skim ricotta cheese, |
| 1 tablespoon unsalted butter | divided |

Insert the crisper plate into the basket and the basket into the unit. Preheat to 175°C. In a 6-by-2-inch round pan, place the pears cut-side up. In a small microwave-safe bowl, melt the honey, butter, and cinnamon. Brush this mixture over the cut sides of the pears. Pour 3 tablespoons of water around the pears in the pan. Once the unit is preheated, place the pan into the basket. After about 18 minutes, check the pears. They should be tender when pierced with a fork and slightly crisp on the edges. If not, resume cooking. When the cooking is complete, baste the pears once with the liquid in the pan. Carefully remove the pears from the pan and place on a serving plate. Drizzle each with some liquid from the pan, sprinkle the walnuts on top, and serve with a spoonful of ricotta cheese.

## Butter and Chocolate Chip Cookies

**Prep time: 20 minutes | Cook time: 11 minutes | Serves 8**

| | |
|---|---|
| 110 g unsalted butter, at room temperature | 35 g cocoa powder, unsweetened |
| 155 g powdered sweetener | 1 ½ teaspoons baking powder |
| 60 g chunky peanut butter | ¼ teaspoon ground cinnamon |
| 1 teaspoon vanilla paste | ¼ teaspoon ginger |
| 1 fine almond flour | 85 g unsweetened, or dark chocolate chips |
| 75 g coconut flour | |

In a mixing dish, beat the butter and sweetener until creamy and uniform. Stir in the peanut butter and vanilla. In another mixing dish, thoroughly combine the flour, cocoa powder, baking powder, cinnamon, and ginger. Add the flour mixture to the peanut butter mixture; mix to combine well. Afterwards, fold in the chocolate chips. Drop by large spoonsful onto a baking paper-lined air fryer basket. Bake at 185ºC for 11 minutes or until golden brown on the top. Bon appétit!

## Strawberry Pecan Pie

**Prep time: 15 minutes | Cook time: 10 minutes | Serves 6**

| | |
|---|---|
| 190 g whole shelled pecans | 12 medium fresh strawberries, hulled |
| 1 tablespoon unsalted butter, softened | 2 tablespoons sour cream |
| 240 ml heavy whipping cream | |

Place pecans and butter into a food processor and pulse ten times until a dough forms. Press dough into the bottom of an ungreased round nonstick baking dish. Place dish into air fryer basket. Adjust the temperature to 160ºC and set the timer for 10 minutes. Crust will be firm and golden when done. Let cool 20 minutes. In a large bowl, whisk cream until fluffy and doubled in size, about 2 minutes. In a separate large bowl, mash strawberries until mostly liquid. Fold strawberries and sour cream into whipped cream. Spoon mixture into cooled crust, cover, and place in refrigerator for at least 30 minutes to set. Serve chilled.

## Pineapple Wontons

**Prep time: 15 minutes | Cook time: 15 to 18 minutes per batch | Serves 5**

| | |
|---|---|
| 225 g cream cheese | 20 wonton wrappers |
| 170 g finely chopped fresh pineapple | Cooking oil spray |

In a small microwave-safe bowl, heat the cream cheese in the microwave on high power for 20 seconds to soften. In a medium bowl, stir together the cream cheese and pineapple until mixed well. Lay out the wonton wrappers on a work surface. A clean table or large cutting board works well. Spoon 1½ teaspoons of the cream cheese mixture onto each wrapper. Be careful not to overfill. Fold each wrapper diagonally across to form a triangle. Bring the 2 bottom corners up toward each other. Do not close the wrapper yet. Bring up the 2 open sides and push out any air. Squeeze the

open edges together to seal. Insert the crisper plate into the basket and the basket into the unit. Preheat the air fryer to 200ºC. Once the unit is preheated, spray the crisper plate with cooking oil. Place the wontons into the basket. You can work in batches or stack the wontons. Spray the wontons with the cooking oil. Cook wontons for 10 minutes, then remove the basket, flip each wonton, and spray them with more oil. Reinsert the basket to resume cooking for 5 to 8 minutes more until the wontons are light golden brown and crisp. If cooking in batches, remove the cooked wontons from the basket and repeat steps 7 and 8 for the remaining wontons. 1When the cooking is complete, cool for 5 minutes before serving.

## Zucchini Bread

**Prep time: 10 minutes | Cook time: 40 minutes | Serves 12**

| | |
|---|---|
| 220 g coconut flour | 1 teaspoon vanilla extract |
| 2 teaspoons baking powder | 3 eggs, beaten |
| 150 g granulated sweetener | 1 courgette, grated |
| 120 ml coconut oil, melted | 1 teaspoon ground cinnamon |
| 1 teaspoon apple cider vinegar | |

In the mixing bowl, mix coconut flour with baking powder, sweetener, coconut oil, apple cider vinegar, vanilla extract, eggs, courgette, and ground cinnamon. Transfer the mixture into the air fryer basket and flatten it in the shape of the bread. Cook the bread at 175ºC for 40 minutes.

## Chocolate Chip Pecan Biscotti

**Prep time: 15 minutes | Cook time: 20 to 22 minutes | Serves 10**

| | |
|---|---|
| 135 g finely ground blanched almond flour | 1 large egg, beaten |
| ¾ teaspoon baking powder | 1 teaspoon pure vanilla extract |
| ½ teaspoon xanthan gum | 50 g chopped pecans |
| ¼ teaspoon sea salt | 40 g organic chocolate chips, |
| 3 tablespoons unsalted butter, at room temperature | Melted organic chocolate chips and chopped pecans, for topping (optional) |
| 35 g powdered sweetener | |

In a large bowl, combine the almond flour, baking powder, xanthan gum, and salt. Line a cake pan that fits inside your air fryer with baking paper. In the bowl of a stand mixer, beat together the butter and powdered sweetener. Add the beaten egg and vanilla and beat for about 3 minutes. Add the almond flour mixture to the butter and egg mixture; beat until just combined. Stir in the pecans and chocolate chips. Transfer the dough to the prepared pan and press it into the bottom. Set the air fryer to 165ºC and bake for 12 minutes. Remove from the air fryer and let cool for 15 minutes. Using a sharp knife, cut the cookie into thin strips, then return the strips to the cake pan with the bottom sides facing up. Set the air fryer to 150ºC. Bake for 8 to 10 minutes. Remove from the air fryer and let cool completely on a wire rack. If desired, dip one side of each biscotti piece into melted chocolate chips, and top with chopped pecans.

## Homemade Mint Pie

**Prep time: 15 minutes | Cook time: 25 minutes | Serves 2**

| | |
|---|---|
| 1 tablespoon instant coffee | 1 teaspoon dried mint |
| 2 tablespoons almond butter, softened | 3 eggs, beaten |
| 2 tablespoons granulated sweetener | 1 teaspoon dried spearmint |
| | 4 teaspoons coconut flour |
| | Cooking spray |

Spray the air fryer basket with cooking spray. Then mix all ingredients in the mixer bowl. When you get a smooth mixture, transfer it in the air fryer basket. Flatten it gently. Cook the pie at 185ºC for 25 minutes.

## Pineapple Galette

**Prep time: 15 minutes | Cook time: 40 minutes | Serves 2**

| | |
|---|---|
| ¼ medium-size pineapple, peeled, cored, and cut crosswise into ¼-inch-thick slices | Finely grated zest of ½ lime |
| 2 tablespoons dark rum, or apple juice | 1 store-bought sheet puff pastry, cut into an 8-inch round |
| 1 teaspoon vanilla extract | 3 tablespoons granulated sugar |
| ½ teaspoon kosher, or coarse sea salt | 2 tablespoons unsalted butter, cubed and chilled |
| | Coconut ice cream, for serving |

In a small bowl, combine the pineapple slices, rum, vanilla, salt, and lime zest and let stand for at least 10 minutes to allow the pineapple to soak in the rum. Meanwhile, press the puff pastry round into the bottom and up the sides of a cake pan and use the tines of a fork to dock the bottom and sides. Arrange the pineapple slices on the bottom of the pastry in a more or less single layer, then sprinkle with the sugar and dot with the butter. Drizzle with the leftover juices from the bowl. Place the pan in the air fryer and bake at 155ºC until the pastry is puffed and golden brown and the pineapple is lightly caramelized on top, about 40 minutes. Transfer the pan to a wire rack to cool for 15 minutes. Unmold the galette from the pan and serve warm with coconut ice cream.

## Almond Shortbread

**Prep time: 10 minutes | Cook time: 12 minutes | Serves 8**

| | |
|---|---|
| 110 g unsalted butter | 1 teaspoon pure almond extract |
| 100 g granulated sugar | 125 g plain flour |

In bowl of a stand mixer fitted with the paddle attachment, beat the butter and sugar on medium speed until light and fluffy (3 to 4 minutes). Add the almond extract and beat until combined (about 30 seconds). Turn the mixer to low. Add the flour a little at a time and beat for about 2 minutes more until well-incorporated. Pat the dough into an even layer in a baking pan. Place the pan in the air fryer basket. Set the air fryer to 190ºC and bake for 12 minutes. Carefully remove the pan from air fryer basket. While the shortbread is still warm and soft, cut it into 8 wedges. Let cool in the pan on a wire rack for 5 minutes. Remove the wedges from the pan and let cool completely on the rack before serving.

## Coconut Mixed Berry Crisp

**Prep time: 5 minutes | Cook time: 20 minutes | Serves 6**

| | |
|---|---|
| 1 tablespoon butter, melted | ½ teaspoon ground cinnamon |
| 340 g mixed berries | ¼ teaspoon ground cloves |
| 65 g granulated sweetener | ¼ teaspoon grated nutmeg |
| 1 teaspoon pure vanilla extract | 50 g coconut chips, for garnish |

Preheat the air fryer to 165ºC. Coat a baking pan with melted butter. Put the remaining ingredients except the coconut chips in the prepared baking pan. Bake in the preheated air fryer for 20 minutes. Serve garnished with the coconut chips.

## Spiced Apple Cake

**Prep time: 15 minutes | Cook time: 30 minutes | Serves 6**

| | |
|---|---|
| Vegetable oil | 1 tablespoon apple pie spice |
| 2 diced & peeled Gala apples | ½ teaspoon ground ginger |
| 1 tablespoon fresh lemon juice | ¼ teaspoon ground cardamom |
| 55 g unsalted butter, softened | ¼ teaspoon ground nutmeg |
| 65 g granulated sugar | ½ teaspoon kosher, or coarse sea salt |
| 2 large eggs | |
| 155 g plain flour | 60 ml whole milk |
| 1½ teaspoons baking powder | Icing sugar, for dusting |

Grease a 0.7-liter Bundt, or tube pan with oil; set aside. In a medium bowl, toss the apples with the lemon juice until well coated; set aside. In a large bowl, combine the butter and sugar. Beat with an electric hand mixer on medium speed until the sugar has dissolved. Add the eggs and beat until fluffy. Add the flour, baking powder, apple pie spice, ginger, cardamom, nutmeg, salt, and milk. Mix until the batter is thick but pourable. Pour the batter into the prepared pan. Top batter evenly with the apple mixture. Place the pan in the air fryer basket. Set the air fryer to 175ºC and cook for 30 minutes, or until a toothpick inserted in the center of the cake comes out clean. Close the air fryer and let the cake rest for 10 minutes. Turn the cake out onto a wire rack and cool completely. Right before serving, dust the cake with icing sugar.

## Apple Wedges with Apricots

**Prep time: 5 minutes | Cook time: 15 to 18 minutes | Serves 4**

| | |
|---|---|
| 4 large apples, peeled and sliced into 8 wedges | 1 to 2 tablespoons granulated sugar |
| 2 tablespoons light olive oil | ½ teaspoon ground cinnamon |
| 95 g dried apricots, chopped | |

Preheat the air fryer to 180ºC. Toss the apple wedges with the olive oil in a mixing bowl until well coated. Place the apple wedges in the air fryer basket and air fry for 12 to 15 minutes. Sprinkle with the dried apricots and air fry for another 3 minutes. Meanwhile, thoroughly combine the sugar and cinnamon in a small bowl. Remove the apple wedges from the basket to a plate. Serve sprinkled with the sugar mixture.

## Fried Cheesecake Bites

**Prep time: 30 minutes | Cook time: 2 minutes |**

**Makes 16 bites**

225 g cream cheese, softened
50 g powdered sweetener, plus
2 tablespoons, divided
4 tablespoons heavy cream,

divided
½ teaspoon vanilla extract
50 g almond flour

In a stand mixer fitted with a paddle attachment, beat the cream cheese, 50 g of the sweetener, 2 tablespoons of the heavy cream, and the vanilla until smooth. Using a small ice-cream scoop, divide the mixture into 16 balls and arrange them on a rimmed baking sheet lined with baking paper. Freeze for 45 minutes until firm. Line the air fryer basket with baking paper and preheat the air fryer to 175ºC. In a small shallow bowl, combine the almond flour with the remaining 2 tablespoons of sweetener. In another small shallow bowl, place the remaining 2 tablespoons cream. One at a time, dip the frozen cheesecake balls into the cream and then roll in the almond flour mixture, pressing lightly to form an even coating. Arrange the balls in a single layer in the air fryer basket, leaving room between them. Air fry for 2 minutes until the coating is lightly browned.

## Lemon Raspberry Muffins

**Prep time: 5 minutes | Cook time: 15 minutes | Serves 6**

220 g almond flour
75 g powdered sweetener
1¼ teaspoons baking powder
⅓ teaspoon ground allspice
⅓ teaspoon ground star anise
½ teaspoon grated lemon zest

¼ teaspoon salt
2 eggs
240 ml sour cream
120 ml coconut oil
60 g raspberries

Preheat the air fryer to 175ºC. Line a muffin pan with 6 paper cases. In a mixing bowl, mix the almond flour, sweetener, baking powder, allspice, star anise, lemon zest, and salt. In another mixing bowl, beat the eggs, sour cream, and coconut oil until well mixed. Add the egg mixture to the flour mixture and stir to combine. Mix in the raspberries. Scrape the batter into the prepared muffin cups, filling each about three-quarters full. Bake for 15 minutes, or until the tops are golden and a toothpick inserted in the middle comes out clean. Allow the muffins to cool for 10 minutes in the muffin pan before removing and serving.

## Olive Oil Cake

**Prep time: 10 minutes | Cook time: 30 minutes | Serves 8**

120 g blanched finely ground almond flour
5 large eggs, whisked
175 ml extra-virgin olive oil

75 g granulated sweetener
1 teaspoon vanilla extract
1 teaspoon baking powder

In a large bowl, mix all ingredients. Pour batter into an ungreased round nonstick baking dish. Place dish into air fryer basket. Adjust the temperature to 150ºC and bake for 30 minutes. The cake will be golden on top and firm in the center when done. Let cake cool in dish 30 minutes before slicing and serving.

## S'mores

**Prep time: 5 minutes | Cook time: 30 seconds |**

**Makes 8 s'mores**

Coconut, or avocado oil, for spraying
8 digestive biscuits

2 (45 g) chocolate bars
4 large marshmallows

Line the air fryer basket with baking paper and spray lightly with oil. Place 4 biscuits into the prepared basket. Break the chocolate bars in half, and place 1/2 on top of each biscuit. Top with 1 marshmallow. Air fry at 190ºC for 30 seconds, or until the marshmallows are puffed, golden brown and slightly melted. Top with the remaining biscuits and serve.

## Lime Bars

**Prep time: 10 minutes | Cook time: 33 minutes |**

**Makes 12 bars**

140 g blanched finely ground almond flour, divided
75 g powdered sweetener, divided

4 tablespoons salted butter, melted
120 ml fresh lime juice
2 large eggs, whisked

In a medium bowl, mix together 110 g flour, 25 g sweetener, and butter. Press mixture into bottom of an ungreased round nonstick cake pan. Place pan into air fryer basket. Adjust the temperature to 150ºC and bake for 13 minutes. Crust will be brown and set in the middle when done. Allow to cool in pan 10 minutes. In a medium bowl, combine remaining flour, remaining sweetener, lime juice, and eggs. Pour mixture over cooled crust and return to air fryer for 20 minutes. Top will be browned and firm when done. Let cool completely in pan, about 30 minutes, then chill covered in the refrigerator 1 hour. Serve chilled.

## Bourbon Bread Pudding

**Prep time: 10 minutes | Cook time: 20 minutes | Serves 4**

3 slices whole grain bread, cubed
1 large egg
240 ml whole milk
2 tablespoons bourbon, or peach juice

½ teaspoons vanilla extract
4 tablespoons maple syrup, divided
½ teaspoons ground cinnamon
2 teaspoons sparkling sugar

Preheat the air fryer to 130ºC. Spray a baking pan with nonstick cooking spray, then place the bread cubes in the pan. In a medium bowl, whisk together the egg, milk, bourbon, vanilla extract, 3 tablespoons of maple syrup, and cinnamon. Pour the egg mixture over the bread and press down with a spatula to coat all the bread, then sprinkle the sparkling sugar on top and bake for 20 minutes. Remove the pudding from the air fryer and allow to cool in the pan on a wire rack for 10 minutes. Drizzle the remaining 1 tablespoon of maple syrup on top. Slice and serve warm.

## Gingerbread

**Prep time: 5 minutes | Cook time: 20 minutes | Makes 1 loaf**

| | |
|---|---|
| Cooking spray | ⅛ teaspoon salt |
| 125 g plain flour | 1 egg |
| 2 tablespoons granulated sugar | 70 g treacle |
| ¾ teaspoon ground ginger | 120 ml buttermilk |
| ¼ teaspoon cinnamon | 2 tablespoons coconut, or |
| 1 teaspoon baking powder | avocado oil |
| ½ teaspoon baking soda | 1 teaspoon pure vanilla extract |

Preheat the air fryer to 165°C. Spray a baking dish lightly with cooking spray. In a medium bowl, mix together all the dry ingredients. In a separate bowl, beat the egg. Add treacle, buttermilk, oil, and vanilla and stir until well mixed. Pour liquid mixture into dry ingredients and stir until well blended. Pour batter into baking dish and bake for 20 minutes, or until toothpick inserted in center of loaf comes out clean.

## Caramelized Fruit Skewers

**Prep time: 10 minutes | Cook time: 3 to 5 minutes | Serves 4**

| | |
|---|---|
| 2 peaches, peeled, pitted, and thickly sliced | ½ teaspoon ground cinnamon |
| 3 plums, halved and pitted | ¼ teaspoon ground allspice |
| 3 nectarines, halved and pitted | Pinch cayenne pepper |
| 1 tablespoon honey | Special Equipment: |
| | 8 metal skewers |

Preheat the air fryer to 200°C. Thread, alternating peaches, plums, and nectarines, onto the metal skewers that fit into the air fryer. Thoroughly combine the honey, cinnamon, allspice, and cayenne in a small bowl. Brush the glaze generously over the fruit skewers. Transfer the fruit skewers to the air fryer basket. You may need to cook in batches to avoid overcrowding. Air fry for 3 to 5 minutes, or until the fruit is caramelized. Remove from the basket and repeat with the remaining fruit skewers. Let the fruit skewers rest for 5 minutes before serving.

## Pumpkin Pudding with Vanilla Wafers

**Prep time: 10 minutes | Cook time: 12 to 17 minutes | Serves 4**

| | |
|---|---|
| 250 g canned no-salt-added pumpkin purée (not pumpkin pie filling) | 1 tablespoon unsalted butter, melted |
| 50 g packed brown sugar | 1 teaspoon pure vanilla extract |
| 3 tablespoons plain flour | 4 low-fat vanilla, or plain wafers, crumbled |
| 1 egg, whisked | Nonstick cooking spray |
| 2 tablespoons milk | |

Preheat the air fryer to 175°C. Coat a baking pan with nonstick cooking spray. Set aside. Mix the pumpkin purée, brown sugar, flour, whisked egg, milk, melted butter, and vanilla in a medium bowl and whisk to combine. Transfer the mixture to the baking pan. Place the baking pan in the air fryer basket and bake for 12 to 17 minutes until set. Remove the pudding from the basket to a wire rack to cool. Divide the pudding into four bowls and serve with the vanilla wafers sprinkled on top.

## Apple Dutch Baby

**Prep time: 30 minutes | Cook time: 16 minutes | Serves 2 to 3**

| Batter: | Apples: |
|---|---|
| 2 large eggs | 2 tablespoon butter |
| 30 g plain flour | 4 tablespoons granulated sugar |
| ¼ teaspoon baking powder | ¼ teaspoon ground cinnamon |
| 1½ teaspoons granulated sugar | ¼ teaspoon ground nutmeg |
| Pinch kosher, or coarse sea salt | 1 small tart apple (such as |
| 120 ml whole milk | Granny Smith), peeled, cored, |
| 1 tablespoon butter, melted | and sliced |
| ½ teaspoon pure vanilla extract | Vanilla ice cream (optional), for |
| ¼ teaspoon ground nutmeg | serving |

For the batter: In a medium bowl, combine the eggs, flour, baking powder, sugar, and salt. Whisk lightly. While whisking continuously, slowly pour in the milk. Whisk in the melted butter, vanilla, and nutmeg. Let the batter stand for 30 minutes. (You can also cover and refrigerate overnight.) For the apples: Place the butter in a baking pan. Place the pan in the air fryer basket. Set the air fryer to 200°C and cook for 2 minutes. In a small bowl, combine 2 tablespoons of the sugar with the cinnamon and nutmeg and stir until well combined. When the pan is hot and the butter is melted, brush some butter up the sides of the pan. Sprinkle the spiced sugar mixture over the butter. Arrange the apple slices in the pan in a single layer and sprinkle the remaining 2 tablespoons sugar over the apples. Keep the air fryer at 200°C and cook for a further2 minutes, or until the mixture bubbles. Gently pour the batter over the apples. Set the air fryer to 175°C cooking for 12 minutes, or until the pancake is golden brown around the edges, the center is cooked through, and a toothpick emerges clean. Serve immediately with ice cream, if desired.

## Crustless Peanut Butter Cheesecake

**Prep time: 10 minutes | Cook time: 10 minutes | Serves 2**

| | |
|---|---|
| 110 g cream cheese, softened | sugar-added peanut butter |
| 2 tablespoons powdered sweetener | ½ teaspoon vanilla extract |
| 1 tablespoon all-natural, no- | 1 large egg, whisked |

In a medium bowl, mix cream cheese and sweetener until smooth. Add peanut butter and vanilla, mixing until smooth. Add egg and stir just until combined. Spoon mixture into an ungreased springform pan and place into air fryer basket. Adjust the temperature to 150°C and bake for 10 minutes. Edges will be firm, but center will be mostly set with only a small amount of jiggle when done. Let pan cool at room temperature 30 minutes, cover with plastic wrap, then place into refrigerator at least 2 hours. Serve chilled.

## Ricotta Lemon Poppy Seed Cake

**Prep time: 10 minutes | Cook time: 55 minutes | Serves 4**

| | |
|---|---|
| Unsalted butter, at room temperature | 55 g coconut oil, melted |
| 110 g almond flour | 2 tablespoons poppy seeds |
| 100 g granulated sugar | 1 teaspoon baking powder |
| 3 large eggs | 1 teaspoon pure lemon extract |
| 55 g heavy cream | Grated zest and juice of 1 |
| 60 g full-fat ricotta cheese | lemon, plus more zest for garnish |

Generously butter a baking pan. Line the bottom of the pan with baking paper cut to fit. In a large bowl, combine the almond flour, sugar, eggs, cream, ricotta, coconut oil, poppy seeds, baking powder, lemon extract, lemon zest, and lemon juice. Beat with a hand mixer on medium speed, until well blended and fluffy. Pour the batter into the prepared pan. Cover the pan tightly with aluminum foil. Set the pan in the air fryer basket. Set the air fryer to 165°C and cook for 45 minutes. Remove the foil and cook for 10 to 15 minutes more, until a knife (do not use a toothpick) inserted into the center of the cake comes out clean. Let the cake cool in the pan on a wire rack for 10 minutes. Remove the cake from pan and let it cool on the rack for 15 minutes before slicing. Top with additional lemon zest, slice and serve.

## Grilled Pineapple Dessert

**Prep time: 5 minutes | Cook time: 12 minutes | Serves 4**

| | |
|---|---|
| Coconut, or avocado oil for misting, or cooking spray | juice |
| 4½-inch-thick slices fresh pineapple, core removed | 2 tablespoons slivered almonds, toasted |
| 1 tablespoon honey | Vanilla frozen yogurt, coconut sorbet, or ice cream |
| ¼ teaspoon brandy, or apple | |

Spray both sides of pineapple slices with oil or cooking spray. Place into air fryer basket. Air fry at 200°C for 6 minutes. Turn slices over and cook for an additional 6 minutes. Mix together the honey and brandy. Remove cooked pineapple slices from air fryer, sprinkle with toasted almonds, and drizzle with honey mixture. Serve with a scoop of frozen yogurt or sorbet on the side.

## Mixed Berry Hand Pies

**Prep time: 5 minutes | Cook time: 30 minutes | Serves 4**

| | |
|---|---|
| 150 g granulated sugar | two equal portions |
| ½ teaspoon ground cinnamon | 1 teaspoon water |
| 1 tablespoon cornflour | 1 package refrigerated |
| 150 g blueberries | shortcrust pastry (or your own homemade pastry) |
| 150 g blackberries | |
| 150 g raspberries, divided into | 1 egg, beaten |

Combine the sugar, cinnamon, and cornstarch in a small saucepan. Add the blueberries, blackberries, and ½ of the raspberries. Toss the berries gently to coat them evenly. Add the teaspoon of water to the saucepan and turn the stovetop on to medium-high heat, stirring occasionally. Once the berries break down, release their juice, and start to simmer (about 5 minutes), simmer for another couple of minutes and then transfer the mixture to a bowl, stir in the remaining ½ of the raspberries and let it cool. Preheat the air fryer to 190°C. Cut the pie dough into four 5-inch circles and four 6-inch circles. Spread the 6-inch circles on a flat surface. Divide the berry filling between all four circles. Brush the perimeter of the dough circles with a little water. Place the 5-inch circles on top of the filling and press the perimeter of the dough circles together to seal. Roll the edges of the bottom circle up over the top circle to make a crust around the filling. Press a fork around the crust to make decorative indentations and to seal the crust shut. Brush the pies with egg wash and sprinkle a little sugar on top. Poke a small hole in the center of each pie with a paring knife to vent the dough. Air fry two pies at a time. Brush or spray the air fryer basket with oil and place the pies into the basket. Air fry for 9 minutes. Turn the pies over and air fry for another 6 minutes. Serve warm or at room temperature.

## Funnel Cake

**Prep time: 10 minutes | Cook time: 5 minutes | Serves 4**

| | |
|---|---|
| Coconut, or avocado oil, for spraying | 240 ml fat-free vanilla Greek yogurt |
| 110 g self-raising flour, plus more for dusting | ½ teaspoon ground cinnamon |
| | ¼ cup icing sugar |

Preheat the air fryer to 190°C. Line the air fryer basket with baking paper, and spray lightly with oil. In a large bowl, mix together the flour, yogurt and cinnamon until the mixture forms a ball. Place the dough on a lightly floured work surface and knead for about 2 minutes. Cut the dough into 4 equal pieces, then cut each of those into 6 pieces. You should have 24 pieces in total. Roll the pieces into 8- to 10-inch-long ropes. Loosely mound the ropes into 4 piles of 6 ropes. Place the dough piles in the prepared basket, and spray liberally with oil. You may need to work in batches, depending on the size of your air fryer. Cook for 5 minutes, or until lightly browned. Dust with the icing sugar before serving.

## Mixed Berries with Pecan Streusel Topping

**Prep time: 5 minutes | Cook time: 17 minutes | Serves 3**

| | |
|---|---|
| 75 g mixed berries | 2 tablespoons chopped walnuts |
| Cooking spray | 3 tablespoons granulated sweetener |
| Topping: | |
| 1 egg, beaten | 2 tablespoons cold salted butter, cut into pieces |
| 3 tablespoons almonds, slivered | |
| 3 tablespoons chopped pecans | ½ teaspoon ground cinnamon |

Preheat the air fryer to 170°C. Lightly spray a baking dish with cooking spray. Make the topping: In a medium bowl, stir together the beaten egg, nuts, sweetener, butter, and cinnamon until well blended. Put the mixed berries in the bottom of the baking dish and spread the topping over the top. Bake in the preheated air fryer for 17 minutes, or until the fruit is bubbly and topping is golden brown. Allow to cool for 5 to 10 minutes before serving.

## Maple-Pecan Tart with Sea Salt

**Prep time: 15 minutes | Cook time: 25 minutes | Serves 8**

| | |
|---|---|
| Tart Crust: | 4 tablespoons unsalted butter, |
| Vegetable oil spray | diced |
| 75 g unsalted butter, softened | 95 g packed brown sugar |
| 50 g firmly packed brown sugar | 60 ml pure maple syrup |
| 125 g plain flour | 60 ml whole milk |
| ¼ teaspoon kosher, or coarse | ¼ teaspoon pure vanilla extract |
| sea salt | 190 g finely chopped pecans |
| Filling: | ¼ teaspoon flaked sea salt |

For the crust: Line a baking pan with foil, leaving a couple of inches of overhang. Spray the foil with vegetable oil spray. In a medium bowl, combine the butter and brown sugar. Beat with an electric mixer on medium-low speed until light and fluffy. Add the flour and kosher salt and beat until the ingredients are well blended. Transfer the mixture (it will be crumbly) to the prepared pan. Press it evenly into the bottom of the pan. Place the pan in the air fryer basket. Set the air fryer to 175°C and cook for 13 minutes. When the crust has 5 minutes left to cook, start the filling. For the filling: In a medium saucepan, combine the butter, brown sugar, maple syrup, and milk. Bring to a simmer, stirring occasionally. When it begins simmering, cook for 1 minute. Remove from the heat and stir in the vanilla and pecans. Carefully pour the filling evenly over the crust, gently spreading with a rubber spatula so the nuts and liquid are evenly distributed. Keep the air fryer at 175°C and cook for 12 minutes, or until mixture is bubbling. (The center should still be slightly jiggly; it will thicken as it cools.) Remove the pan from the air fryer and sprinkle the tart with the sea salt. Cool completely on a wire rack until room temperature. Transfer the pan to the refrigerator to chill. When cold (the tart will be easier to cut), use the foil overhang to remove the tart from the pan and cut into 8 wedges. Serve at room temperature.

## Coconut-Custard Pie

**Prep time: 10 minutes | Cook time: 20 to 23 minutes | Serves 4**

| | |
|---|---|
| 240 ml milk | 2 eggs |
| 50 g granulated sugar, plus 2 | 2 tablespoons melted butter |
| tablespoons | Cooking spray |
| 30 g scone mix | 50 g desiccated, sweetened |
| 1 teaspoon vanilla extract | coconut |

Place all ingredients except coconut in a medium bowl. Using a hand mixer, beat on high speed for 3 minutes. Let sit for 5 minutes.

Preheat the air fryer to 165°C. Spray a baking pan with cooking spray and place pan in air fryer basket. Pour filling into pan and sprinkle coconut over top. Cook pie for 20 to 23 minutes or until center sets.

## Luscious Coconut Pie

**Prep time: 5 minutes | Cook time: 45 minutes | Serves 6**

| | |
|---|---|
| 100 g desiccated, unsweetened | 1½ teaspoons vanilla extract |
| coconut, plus 25 g, divided | ¼ teaspoon salt |
| 2 eggs | 2 tablespoons powdered |
| 355 ml almond milk | sweetener (optional) |
| 100 g granulated sweetener | 120 g whipping cream, whipped |
| 55 g coconut flour | until stiff (optional) |
| 55 g unsalted butter, melted | |

Spread 25 g of the coconut in the bottom of a pie plate and place in the air fryer basket. Set the air fryer to 175°C and air fry the coconut while the air fryer preheats, about 5 minutes, until golden brown. Transfer the coconut to a small bowl and set aside for garnish. Brush the pie plate with oil and set aside. In a large bowl, combine the remaining 100 g shredded coconut, eggs, milk, granulated sweetener, coconut flour, butter, vanilla, and salt. Whisk until smooth. Pour the batter into the prepared pie plate and air fry for 40 to 45 minutes, or until a toothpick inserted into the center of the pie comes out clean. (Check halfway through the baking time and rotate the pan, if necessary, for even baking.) Remove the pie from the air fryer and place on a baking rack to cool completely. Garnish with the reserved toasted coconut and the powdered sweetener or whipped cream, if desired. Cover and refrigerate leftover pie for up to 3 days.

## Pecan Brownies

**Prep time: 10 minutes | Cook time: 20 minutes | Serves 6**

| | |
|---|---|
| 50 g blanched finely ground | 55 g unsalted butter, softened |
| almond flour | 1 large egg |
| 55 g powdered sweetener | 35 g chopped pecans |
| 2 tablespoons unsweetened | 40 g low-carb, sugar-free |
| cocoa powder | chocolate chips |
| ½ teaspoon baking powder | |

In a large bowl, mix almond flour, sweetener, cocoa powder, and baking powder. Stir in butter and egg. Fold in pecans and chocolate chips. Scoop mixture into a round baking pan. Place pan into the air fryer basket. Adjust the temperature to 150°C and bake for 20 minutes. When fully cooked a toothpick inserted in center will come out clean. Allow 20 minutes to fully cool and firm up.

Printed in Great Britain
by Amazon

16434761R00038